Pierre Laffitte

A General View of Chinese Civilization and of the Relations

of the West with China

Pierre Laffitte

A General View of Chinese Civilization and of the Relations of the West with China

ISBN/EAN: 9783337003975

Printed in Europe, USA, Canada, Australia, Japan

Cover: Foto ©Suzi / pixelio.de

More available books at **www.hansebooks.com**

A GENERAL VIEW

OF

CHINESE CIVILIZATION

AND OF

THE RELATIONS OF THE WEST WITH CHINA.

FROM THE FRENCH OF

M. PIERRE LAFFITTE;

(DIRECTOR OF POSITIVISM).

TRANSLATED BY

JOHN CAREY HALL, M.A.,

ASSISTANT JAPANESE SECRETARY TO H. B. M.'s LEGATION, TŌKYŌ.

Progress is the development of Order.
—Auguste Comte.

LONDON:
TRÜBNER & Co., LUDGATE HILL.

YOKOHAMA, SHANGHAI & HONGKONG:
KELLY & WALSH (LIMITED).

TŌKYŌ & YOKOHAMA:
Z. P. MARUYA & Co. (LIMITED).

1887.

INTRODUCTION.

In 1859 and 1860 I delivered a course of free public lectures on the General History of Humanity.[1] Three of the lectures in that course were devoted to Confucius and Chinese Civilization; and these I now publish.

My main object in singling out this particular portion of a vast body of doctrine for separate publication is to bring to the notice of the higher minds and hearts amongst us the need there is for setting on foot a reasonable and moral policy for regulating the relations of the West with the rest of the World. Those relations are coming more and more under the direction of a commercialism of the baser sort, or of a narrow proselytism, which is often, after all, very little better than a pretext for furthering some political or mercantile object. I am in hopes, also, that this sample of a political conception, based on a thorough philosophic study of the situation which it is desired to modify, will suffice to convince reflecting minds of the necessity of bringing to the study of social phenomena at least the same degree of attention and perseverance as is required for the study of the simpler phenomena of life and of the world. Moreover, the institution of a policy which embraces in its scope the whole extent of our planet, is not only an object of high importance, in itself, but is also connected, both directly and indirectly, with the more pressing needs of the reorganization of the West:

[1] The program of the course is published at the end of this volume, by way of giving a general idea of its scope. For fuller details, see the opening lecture, published by Dunod, quai des Augustins 49, Paris, in 1 vol. 8vo, entitled *Philosophic Course on the General History of Humanity*, by M. Pierre Laffitte.

for the true doctrine, fit to usher in the normal state of Humanity, should show itself able at the outset to construct a policy that really embraces the whole sum of terrestrial affairs. This is what Positivism actually does, as will be seen before very long by those whose minds are capable of appreciating the value of such a doctrine, destined, as it is, to form the bond of union of the noble hearts of every land.

But before the group formed by the advanced populations can adopt a proper policy towards the rest of the world, a change must be brought about in its way of looking at itself. When that change does take place, it will have the further effect of producing a wholesome reaction on the internal politics of the West.

This change consists in dropping the notion of *Christendom*, and adopting in place of it, the notion of *Westerndom* or *The West*. Such a substitution, being nothing more than the systematic expression of a fact, will be welcomed by all serious and reflecting minds. Only a few fanatics will object to the change.

By the term *Westerndom*, or the *Western Commonwealth*, I mean to indicate the group of the five leading peoples, the French in the centre, the Italian and Spanish to the South, the British and the German to the North, who, as pointed out by Auguste Comte, have been united by the same interests and responsibilities since the time of Charlemagne.

The West, is a more rational term than *Christendom*. To begin with, it is more precise, for it eliminates from such a group both Russia and the Christian peoples of the East, who cannot be seriously imagined to belong to it. Another advantage it has is that it represents fully the whole set of antecedents that have helped to mould this memorable group. The word *Christian* points only to one of those antecedents, a noteworthy and important one no doubt, but, in reality, the least decisive of them all. *Westerndom* owes its formation to its conquest by the Romans more than to anything else; and the formative process was completed by the policy of Charlemagne, by the sway of the Catholic Church, by the incomparable influence of Feudalism, and the revolutionary developments of the last five centuries. This term has thus the advantage of allowing their due to all our ancestors; whereas the other ignores the more important of them in favour of one alone.

But apart from its being the more sensible term, the substitution of *Westerndom* for *Christendom*, must bring about a great change in the views of statesmen, and, in the end, in the views of peoples also, by placing them at a really civic point of view. The civic standpoint, obscured since the days of Cæsar and Trajan beneath the stratum of Christianity, cropped out, as it were, in the grand types of Henry the Fourth and Richelieu; but it was only in Frederic the Second, the greatest statesman the West can boast of since the time of Charlemagne, that it came forth into full display. Not that the genius of a Frederic is needed nowadays; the situation is so clear that any real statesman must take it in at a glance. If Frederic was able to govern by placing himself at the purely civic standpoint of a great dictator, what for such a man was then a possibility, is now a necessity. That is to say, a statesman's duty in these days is to govern without any theological bias whatsoever. Theological considerations must henceforth be relegated exclusively to the sphere of private life. Indeed, in France, that is the actual state of the law, resulting from the proclamation of freedom of worship. If, according to the correct saying of a contemporary legist, Law is atheous, we may say with still greater truth that in France the State has no religion. It is for statesmen, therefore, and for peoples, to place their ideas and their sentiments on a level with the situation.

This substitution of *Westerndom* for *Christendom*, so vital for the internal state of the West as marking out the only common ground on which all can agree, will have a no less efficacious influence on its external policy. Henceforward it will be impossible for the West to aim at foisting upon the East a synthesis that is in utter decay at home. The conception capable of becoming the universal religion must be sought for outside of all the provisional syntheses. This Christian point of view, which so profoundly vitiates our appreciation of the other peoples of the world, will then no longer form a barrier to our understanding them aright. It will thenceforth be possible to judge of them rationally, unbiassed by retrograde or revolutionary prejudices.

These general views are such as can now be accepted in the West by all superior minds; by all those, in a word, who are fit to deal with social questions. It is not too much to say that, on this head, current opinions are beneath the requirements of the situation, to a degree perhaps unparalleled in history.

I have endeavoured to bring out clearly the superiority of the religious spirit, by contrasting the admirable mission organized by the Jesuits with the oppression, sometimes hypocritical, sometimes violent, set on foot by an ignoble mercantilism.[1]

I venture to hope, indeed, that truly religious natures, especially Catholics, will give their support to a rational and moral policy which reprobates the employment of public force in the service of private greed, and which comes forward, in the name of Humanity, to claim a suitable respect for the civilizations that have arisen on the planet outside of the boundaries of the West. Every religion worthy of the name, be its dogmatic basis what it may, is bound to protest aloud against the employment of force either as a prelude or as a support to preaching. In this respect the noble mission of the Jesuits in China should be taken as a pattern.

Finally, we may hope that some day the healthy public

---

[1] The allusion is, of course, to the opium trade.—*Tr.*

opinion of the West will bring about, under the name of the *Navy of the West*, the establishment of a public force which, besides safeguarding a useful commerce, shall be specially employed in protecting the backward populations against attempts at oppression which are all the more certain to ensue as the cupidity in which they originate will be less and less under control.

In the work I now publish I have been inspired not only by the leading principles of the Positive Philosophy but also by the special view, as profound as it is luminous, put forward by Auguste Comte on the subject of Chinese civilization :—

"A special set of influences, mostly social, caused Chinese "civilization to develop Fetishism to a far higher degree than "was possible elsewhere. Better systematized than in any other "case, it there prevailed over Theologism, and preserved a third "of our species from the system of castes, in spite of the fact "that callings were hereditary," etc.—(*Auguste Comte: Synthèse Subjective, Vol. 1, Introduction.*)

Such is the inspiration under which, in my course of public lectures on *The General History of Humanity*, I have considered the civilization of China and its most eminent representative, Confucius.

I venture to hope that such a work will help to disseminate the conviction that the Demonstrated Religion alone can encompass the sum of terrestrial affairs in a policy at once rational and moral.

P. LAFFITTE,
10, rue Monsieur-le-Prince.

PARIS, *27th Saint Paul, 73 (15th June, 1861).*

TABLE OF CONTENTS.

A GENERAL SURVEY

CHINESE CIVILIZATION

AND OF

THE RELATIONS OF THE WEST WITH CHINA.

FIRST LECTURE.

(THE FOURTEENTH OF THE COURSE.)

FRIDAY, 6TH HOMER, 72—3RD FEBRUARY, 1860.

ABSTRACT ESTIMATE OF THE ESSENTIAL BASES OF CHINESE CIVILIZATION AND OF THE ELEMENTS THAT HAVE MODIFIED IT.

GENTLEMEN,—We are to enter to-day upon a survey of the whole field of Chinese civilization. In view of the importance of such a study, both in itself and in its bearings on the problems of the science of society, we shall devote to it three lectures.

At the base of the farthest East is a noteworthy civilization, which, say what we may about it, is in constant development and in full activity, and is being brought day by day into closer contact with the the West. This civilization, in so many respects so much misunderstood, is that of China. In a philosophic point of view it will be of high importance to make a study of it, on account of the strange appearance it has presented to nearly all who have concerned themselves to observe it, even when their materials were ample and their disposition towards it all that could be desired. In another point of view the study will be of great usefulness as furnishing to the West a foundation for a truly rational policy.

A

Since the time of the great mission of the Jesuits, Chinese civilization has been the subject of many important works. Up till their time,
Marco Polo's stories had been set down as belonging to the fabulous.
For our first substantial knowledge of China we are indebted, after all, to
the Jesuits; and since that period the investigation of the subject has
been pursued with much ardour and devotion, and, in most cases, with
a real sympathy with the civilization thus studied. Nevertheless, it may
be affirmed, in spite of some very ingenious views and some interesting
special observations, that a general and systematic estimate of that
civilization is a want which yet remains to be supplied.

This is not to be wondered it; for such an estimate was impossible
until after the discovery, made by Auguste Comte, of the abstract laws
of intellectual evolution. Before that, it was not possible for an observer
to place himself at the truly relative point of view, and to completely
divest himself of prepossessions, in dealing with anterior stages of the
human mind.

The intellects of all who have heretofore attempted to study China
have been dominated either by theology, or by metaphysics, or by pure
science. Now, not one of these three frames of mind is fit to estimate,
clearly and completely, the civilization of China.

In the case of the theological spirit, this assertion is self-evident.
What we have here to deal with is a civilization the fundamental basis
of which is not theology; a people who have had no spontaneous
theological development of their own; to whom such a mode of thought
was an importation from abroad at a time when their civilization had
already received its definitive embodiment. Consequently, men like the
Jesuits, for instance, who took an ardent interest in Chinese civilization,
were unable to comprehend anything more than the details of it. They
never understood it as a whole, nor its essential character; and they
consequently used to attribute to Chinese thinkers conceptions of a kind
which, to the minds of the latter, were totally unfamiliar.

As for the metaphysical spirit, its incompetency is still more manifest. Metaphysics being nothing but a gradual and dissolving modification of theology, how could minds dominated by such an influence
judge soundly, and as a whole, a civilization which is still more unfamiliar with metaphysics than with theology? The thing is so utterly

impossible that we have the spectacle of so distinguished a man as Abel Remusat, (whose knowledge of China was so great), mistaking the philosophy of Lao-tse for the representative of the primitive thought of China, the starting point of its civilization. Now, this highly metaphysical philosophy of Lao-tse is, as I shall show, merely a disturbing element, or at any rate only a modifying element, in Chinese civilization; and most certainly an importation from a foreign source. This is a striking example of the power which the prevailing pursuits of the time can exercise over distinguished intellects, even when adequately stored with literary knowledge. At the time when M. Abel Remusat wrote, the philosophic stage was filled by a school of metaphysics which shone with an ephemeral brilliancy, nowadays burnt out. Involuntarily swayed by such a situation, M. Remusat thought to make more attractive the China he had so deeply studied, by displaying there, in their most distant cradle, the discursive flights of metaphysics with which the literary men of Europe were then pre-occupied.

Science, properly so called, was no more fit than theology or metaphysics to furnish a real explanation of this civilization. Yet there are many points at which the scientific spirit and the spirit of this civilization are in accord; mainly in this direction, that both alike acknowledge the spontaneous activity of matter. Still, science was neither sufficiently freed from its metaphysical swaddling bands, nor arrived at a point of view sufficiently general, for the handling of such a problem; and a further hindrance was, that the essentially abstract character of Western science ill-prepared it for comprehending the solid but concrete Chinese spirit. What was needed, therefore, as an indispensable prerequisite for the systematic study of this great problem, was a discovery of the laws which govern the human intelligence. That discovery was made by Auguste Comte. The theory of Chinese civilization furnishes a difficult and characteristic application of the principles of the true philosophy of history.

Before directly entering upon this enquiry, I must first explain the essential difference between Fetishism and Theologism, and show that Theologism is nothing more than a transitional stage of evolution between the primitive Fetishism and the definitive Positivism.

In the evolution of every society there are but two completely normal states that can last and hold together, untroubled by that instability which inseparably attaches to the theological state. These are, on the one hand, the Fetishistic state, the fundamental starting point of human reason and of all sociability whatever ; and, on the other hand, the Positive state, which is their final goal.

After rapidly sketching the essential distinction between Fetishism and Theologism, I shall dwell specially on this cardinal thesis, that Theologism is a mere transition.

Intellectually, Fetishism consists in conceiving bodies as being not only active, but alive ; in supposing the various modes of activity manifested by objects to be due to feelings and desires animating them ; in a word, it consists in assimilating the world to man. In such a mode of thinking there is but one exaggeration committed, and that a simple one, resting on the basis of an incontestable truth. It is a truth, (which science is gradually adopting, and which Positivism has placed beyond doubt), that matter is really active. But besides the activity proper to matter in general, there is a special mode of activity which belongs to certain bodies only ; namely, life. All bodies are active, but all are not alive. The only mistake made by Fetishism, in this connection, is that of attributing to all bodies a mode of activity which belongs only to some. The error lies in conceiving all bodies as endowed, not only with a spontaneous activity,—which is an indisputable fact ; but also as living,—which is an exaggeration, necessary at the outset.

It may be laid down, in fact, that the human mind actually needs such a theory as its starting point. What is the fundamental law according to which our intelligence acts ? It is that of assimilating the phenomena with which we are least familiar to those which we know best ; which amounts to saying that the essential tendency of our mind is to form the most simple hypothesis, having regard to all the particulars given. This capital law of the *First Philosophy* is but the systematic recognition of a great general fact of our intelligence. Now, that of which we have the most and best knowledge to commence with is man. We are conscious of ourselves ; we are aware that our acts are brought about by reason of a set of particular feelings, of distinct impulses, anger, kindness, love, etc. Consequently, when men saw that external bodies act with an intensity very much greater than living bodies themselves; when they saw rivers running and storms raging, and all those grand meteorological phenomena which prove that there is in matter so characteristic and so potent an activity, they must inevitably have supposed that the bodies manifesting that activity will that activity and put it forth in virtue of feelings and fancies similar to those which determine the acts of man. Fetishism, therefore, is actually an inevitable stage of human intelligence; a necessary result of a fundamental tendency of our mind and of the notions or knowledge we have to begin with.

The final term of the Fetishistic stage is astrolatry, properly so called. When, under the influence of this spontaneous Fetishism, aided by favourable cosmological conditions, a society has reached the stage of settled life, and when sufficient means have been provided to enable a certain number of individuals to observe the heavenly bodies and to devote themselves entirely to purely speculative work, then, on the top of the spontaneous popular Fetishism, there is super-induced a more systematic Fetishism, which consists in ascribing to those distant beings a directing power; and attentive observation soon demonstrates that they do really exercise an all-controlling influence. To sum up, then; Fetishism is the necessary starting-point of the human mind; and the final and most systematic element of the Fetishistic stage is the worship of the heavenly bodies.

What are the services rendered to the human mind by Fetishism? Besides being inevitable, (since it is the only theory that could spontaneously arise out of the primitive conditions of our nature and our situation), we owe to it the regular and developed institution of concrete observation, or the observation of beings. In fact, Fetishism conceives each phenomenon as produced by the very will of the being which presents it. This being has thus passions, sentiments and moral dispositions which completely bring it into close relations with the observer. Hence, the image of each of these beings appears with a force, a clearness and an intensity which it cannot have for observers for whom these bodies are quite inert, and devoid of any effective relation to themselves. It is very certain that this close relation of hate, good will, anger, etc., between the being observed and the observer must necessarily produce a more exact image and a more vivid representation. Fetishism, then, institutes concrete observation, that is to say, the observation of beings, with a power all its own, and thus furnishes the concrete images which afterwards serve as the foundation for abstract contemplation, or observation of phenomena. Fetishism thus accumulates the materials of all our speculations of every sort ; and it plays this leading part in the development of each individual as well as in that of the species.

Theologism, of which Polytheism is the most characteristic phase, arises from abstract observation, through the necessary medium of a priesthood. Let me briefly work out this important proposition.

When the human mind has reached the stage of ascertaining the properties common to different bodies and considering them apart, the necessity of representing those properties independently of the bodies to which they belong, impels it, in virtue of the above explained primitive propensity of assimilating all things to man, to invest a particular being with the direction and production of each of those phenomena. Thus, when we rise, for instance, from the notion of an individual tree to the more abstract notion of a forest, we bring in a god of the forest ; that is to say, a being who presides over the whole set of phenomena common to all the various trees of the forest.

Polytheism, or the creation of beings distinct from bodies, yet producing in bodies the various phenomena they manifest, arises from abstract observation ; and when once the logical artifice of imagining gods to represent phenomena, instead of attributing the phenomena to beings, has been adopted, this artifice, susceptible as it is of immense development, methodizes abstraction and allows of the process being repeated without limit.

But this systematic introduction of abstraction, by the creation of gods, is a highly difficult intellectual operation, such as could not emanate spontaneously from the vulgar mind. It is always the work of a distinct class devoted to speculation ; that is to say, to a priesthood ; and, once begun, its very tendency is to promote the development of the priestly class.

Thus, after Fetishism there comes, through the intermediary of a priesthood, Polytheism or Theologism.   Deriving its origin from abstraction, Polytheism goes on to consolidate that mental process and to extend it more and more.

On considering attentively this second characteristic stage of human reason, we are at once struck with the profound mental consistency of Fetishism as compared with the inevitable instability of Polytheism.

Restricted as it is to observation of beings, Fetishism has no room left it for wandering far astray. From what source, then, can it be that the aberrations of the human mind proceed? It is from the institution of abstraction; that is to say, from the consideration of phenomena independently of the bodies by which the phenomena are manifested. The result of that is, that it is possible to conceive the phenomenon, whatever it may be, under an endless variety of conditions different from those under which it is found actually existing. Thus, if we study the phenomenon of locomotion, apart by itself, instead of concentrating our attention upon real bodies in motion, we can soon get so far as to imagine locomotion in an infinity of cases which concrete observation has never made known to us; we can conceive of locomotion on water, or through the air, as an attribute of all existences animate or inanimate; we can conceive of it as possible without any reference to time; that is to say, with infinite quickness. In a word, the abstract study of phenomena allows us to conceive an infinity of possible cases, whereas concrete observation makes known to us only real cases.

The institution of abstraction, due to Polytheism, therefore places the intelligence in an active but unstable situation, where it is always liable to be led very far astray. Fetishism, on the other hand, restricted to observation of beings, and taking account of real cases only, regardless of the possible cases which abstraction makes imaginable, affords a mental stage marked by less activity, indeed, but by a high degree of consistency, and of perfect correctness.

Fetishism is naturally synthetic, for it never looks at phenomena as isolated, but always takes note of their mutual interdependences. But it is not systematic. Systematization always implies previous abstraction. The Fetishistic stage does not allow of the characteristic development of the various essential aspects of our nature. It does not allow, for instance, of the development of the greater science; that is to say, of abstract science, which aims at discovering the real laws, whether of succession or similitude, of the various orders of phenomena. It is only by separating phenomena and considering them, as it were, in isolation that we can hope to find out the laws which govern them. Real scientific development, therefore, necessarily implies the previous establishment of abstraction. That is one of the great aspects of our nature which cannot be developed during the Fetishistic stage. Therefore, although Fetishism is a synthetic state, capable of lasting long, and self-consistent, it does not promote the special culture of the several elements of human nature, nor does it admit of their being truly systematised.

Positivism alone satisfies these two conditions : it is synthetic ; but while, on the one hand, profoundly abstract, it is systematic, and co-ordinates the several special faculties of human nature, after they have been developed by exercise.

It is, then, between primitive Fetishism and definitive Positivism, synthetic and systematic, that Theologism finds its place, constituting a needful stepping-stone for the development of the human forces ; for Positivism cannot regulate those forces until after they have been developed. We must therefore conceive it to be the function of theology to preside over the special evolution of the several elementary powers of human nature ; but, inasmuch as it cannot regulate them, it is necessarily unstable. Theologism, therefore, is merely a transition, more or less rapid, between the primitive state and the final state of the human mind.

This leading proposition has been proved by Auguste Comte in respect of the three grand transitions, the Greek, the Roman and the Feudal. The course of revolutionary change which, in the West, began with the fourteenth century, ought rather to be called a crisis than a transition, in view of the more and more anarchical character it manifests in proportion as it draws nearer to its close. Each one of those transitions has, in a special manner, presided over one of the great aspects of our nature ; the Greek transition over intelligence, the Roman over activity, the Feudal over feeling.

This conception must, it seems to me, be extended to theocracy itself. Every stage of theologism should be regarded as a transition, more or less stable.

We may say, in a general way, that theologism is more or less revolutionary, and that it cannot be other than a passing phase ; for it institutes, but cannot regulate, abstraction.

In fact, it is the theological spirit which gives birth to abstract ideas, representing them by gods, whose wills are, of course, more or less arbitrary. There being no limit to the faculty of forming abstractions in this way, the result is an infinite variety of erratic mental rambling, the only check upon which is that imposed by the necessities of practical life. Theologism, then, is a mental state which is always easily led astray, has never been sufficiently brought under regulation, and has always caused disturbances in the body of institutions amongst which it has arisen. Abstraction can be regulated only by the scientific spirit, which regards all phenomena as subject to invariable laws of succession and similitude.

Thus every theological stage, of what sort soever it may be, is, of necessity, unstable. If, now, we direct our attention to theocracy, properly so called—the first phase of the theological stage—we shall come upon the direct proof of our proposition.

The characteristic of theocracy is the prevalence of caste, and the co-ordination of the various castes amongst themselves by the preponderance of the priestly caste. The regime of castes does, without doubt, effectively give rise to diversity of occupations, stereotyping them as it were; and, by thus consolidating the division of labour, it affords scope for some important developments of our activity. But the co-ordination of the various castes by the priesthood is not sufficiently effective. Indeed we may say—what is the exact contrary of the vulgar prejudice on the point—that theocracy *does not institute a sufficient government;* it is a regime which is not governed enough. In a real theocracy, which must always rest upon Polytheism, there has never been a single condensation of the priesthood, such as there was in the Jewish regime and in the Papacy. There are distinct priestly families, corresponding to the various divinities. That much, indeed, was indispensable; otherwise the oppressiveness of such a regime would have been more intense than we can imagine. But, the various elements of the priestly caste not being grouped round a single over-ruling priest, the consequence is that the sacerdotal caste does not govern enough. It establishes rules as to eating, clothing and so forth ; it consolidates the division of labour; it gives a religious consecration to the hereditary transmission of property; but it fails to organize a sufficient binding

together of the various castes. Hence the internal organization of such
a regime lacks stability. The common prejudice, which regards *too
much government* as its main defect, is therefore the exact opposite of the
truth. Again, as regards societies outside of it, the theocratic regime,
properly so called, is wanting in the power of resistance; or, if this
resisting power be sufficiently developed by the rise of a warrior caste,
the theocratic regime itself is menaced. The soldiers get the upper
hand of the priests, far enough to keep them under control, but not far
enough to bring about the preponderance of the downright military
character, as happened in the case of the civilization of Rome. The
result is, then, a hybrid regime, like that of ancient Persia, for instance,
which, in the ordinary superficial opinion, has been taken as the true
type of a theocracy, whereas it is merely a debased variety of that
regime.

In itself, then, and apart from the drawbacks incident to all forms
of theologism, the theocratic stage of society is found wanting in two
essential points. There is too little of government in it, and too little
power of energetic reaction against external disturbances. It cannot,
therefore, be otherwise than a transitional form, far too unsteady to
last.

This proposition is of real historical importance, since it gives
greater exactitude to our estimates of the various states of society that
have arisen on our planet. It has, moreover, a high social value, since
it establishes a closer relation between the only two religions that have
been and can be universal, Fetishism and Positivism.

Fetishism is the only religion that has been spontaneously universal.
It is the mental state with which all intelligences have made their first
attempts, the starting point of all stages of social organization. Nay,
more, concrete or practical reason continued to be Fetishistic, even in
the civilizations that advanced to the stage of Monotheism. People
even who hold that there is only one God governing all things, explain,
in ordinary life, some kinds of phenomena as being caused by the will,
more or less distinct, of the beings under observation. This concrete
reason, persistently Fetishistic, is the general, universal reason which
sways all intelligence. Abstract reason, which systematises and co-
ordinates, has hitherto had a merely modificatory action. It may be

asserted, then, that the popular masses, during all the stages of social development, have kept Fetishism as the foundation of their mental state.

Fetishism, again, being, in all states of society, the really universal religion, since it is the basis of concrete or practical reason, it was highly important to show that stability is its essential characteristic : whilst, on the contrary, instability is the inherent vice of Theologism, which brings in abstraction without regulating it.   This material proposition will give us a better understanding of what ought to be, and will more and more come to be, the relation between Fetishism, the spontaneously universal religion, and Positivism, the systematically universal religion.   Moreover, Positivism alone, in its own characteristic way, does justice to Fetishism ; it develops it, and finally incorporates it.   It was really worth our while, therefore, to take so much pains, in the beginning of our survey, to put Theologism, as a whole, in its true position, namely, that of a passing interlude between the two fundamental stages of the human reason.

Since the end of last century, as Theologism has been gradually losing its hold over the intellect, even cultivated minds are tending, of their own accord, to turn back towards Fetishism.   This tendency is clearly shown by the development of Fetishistic poetry ; and even the extravagant flights of pantheism are an indistinct but sure indication of this spontaneous inclination of cultivated minds towards Fetishism ; so that in doing justice to it, and giving it a suitable incorporation, Positivism at once meets the requirements of the popular reason and comes forward to systematise a general inclination of the cultivated intellect.

We are now in a position to understand the importance of making a study of Chinese civilization ; a civilization which is Fetishistic to the core, and has developed itself in that course with a steadiness, power and grandeur truly admirable.   The study will, therefore, be highly valuable from the historical point of view.   And it will be of great political and moral importance.   For the relations of the West with China, and indeed with all the other parts of the planet, are tainted with an anarchical and mischief-making immorality.   It is needful that the Religion which is to establish the control of man's powers, the

supremacy of morals over politics, should make such a civilization understood.   In this way Positivism will show its fitness, its exclusive fitness,
for directing the affairs of our world.   Such, I hope, will be the conviction impressed upon your minds, Gentlemen, by the compendious enquiry
we are now to enter upon.

I shall begin with a general estimate of Chinese civilization as a
whole ; first, in its essential elements; then, in its concrete development.

Next, I shall examine the merits of the man who, from the intellectual
and moral point of view, was the loftiest type of that civilization, the
embodiment of its fundamental spirit, and whose name commands the
deep veneration of the people of its vast realm, Confucius.

In the third place, I shall enquire what have been, historically, the
relations of the West with China, and what they ought finally to be.

*Fetishism, systematised by the worship of the sky, is the mental
basis of Chinese civilization :*—Such is the one chief proposition which
must be set forth in the clearest possible light before the true spirit of
that great civilization can be understood.   We have shown that every
society whatsoever must needs begin with Fetishism.   In China, that
stage received a real systematization, which gave it such an immense
consistency and power of growth that it became the basis of the social
evolution of that vast population.   In other countries, Fetishism has left
many unmistakable traces :   in China it has held its ground, lasted and
developed.

When we look, in fact, at the various temples and altars innumer-
able erected in that huge empire, we see that they are dedicated to
rivers, mountains, constellations, to the principal planets, to the Sky, to
the Earth.   The worship of the spirits of the dead is there highly
developed ; familiar to every one, it has been orgainzed by a people
who have no belief in a future life.   Now what are the spirits of the dead
but fetishes, arising from our mortal remains, and which, according to
that point of view, keep on a sort of activity and vitality of their own ?
Death, in the sense in which Theology and Metaphysics conceive it, has
no existence for the Fetishist.   To his eyes, it is merely one mode of
vitality substituted for another.   Hence that contempt for death, which,
as Western believers in Theology themselves bear witness, is so markedly

displayed by a people who, on the other hand, have absolutely no conception of what we mean by a future life. This apparent contradiction Theology admits to be a fact, and yet is unable to explain.

In China, Fetishism has been reduced to system by the *worship of the Sky;* and this systematization dates back to the very origin of the civilization of that empire.

The Sky is, in reality, the preponderant fetish; it is the puissant being whose action co-ordinates the activity of all the others. But its control is only preponderant, *not absolute;* that is a point which it is all-important to note. In Theologism, especially in its monotheistic stage, the supernatural power is absolute, and has an arbitrary will; but it is not so in Fetishism. There the will is preponderant over, but in contact with, and related to, other spontaneous wills, which have their own law, a distinct sort of existence, as it were. In the present case, the preponderating being whose activity co-ordinates and dominates that of all the others, is the Sky. It is on this grand notion that the philosophers and legislators of China have taken their stand, in order to regulate the civilization they had to deal with. We can frame to ourselves an idea of the train of thought by which the legislators reached this systematic conception of the *Sky.*

The Sky is the common seat, visible and evident, of all the heavenly bodies. These heavenly bodies have an intense and indubitable activity. It is certain that human life, throughout its whole extent, is regulated by the course of the most powerful of those bodies, the Sun ; so much so, indeed, that in a great many of the stages of society the Sun became the preponderant fetish. But, if the heavenly bodies have so great an activity, then surely the Sky, their common seat, must be the most powerful of all beings. On this point, M. Remusat has remarked : " It is not to be supposed that the philosophers, any more than the people of China, worship the visible heaven we look upon."[1] Why not ? Is not that more rational than worshiping subjective beings

---

[1] That is just what they do. In fact the Chinese philosophers, who designate heaven or the sky, by the word Tien, designate the Christian god by the word Tien chu ; showing clearly that the Christian conception differs from the Chinese conception in this, that the Christians conceive of a being distinct from heaven, who is outside of it and directs it.

that have never been seen and never will be seen ? Has not this being very great power over us as constituting the seat of the beings which have most influence over our existence ? Is it surprising, then, that they should worship it, that they should consider its activity as preponderant, when direct observation shows that such is the fact ? It is the disposition created in us by the theologico-metaphysical state, and bolstered up by the supposed inertness of matter, that renders men, in so many other respects of extraordinary intelligence, absolutely unable to comprehend Fetishism ; which, after all, is much nearer to science than is Theologism ; since its sole mistake is not distinguishing sufficiently life, properly so called, from activity.

The second great fetish of China, subordinate to the first, is the Earth. To this second systematic element of Chinese Fetishism is allied the worship of rivers, and of mountains ; just as the worship of the moon, of the planets and of the constellations is allied to that of the Sky.

The Earth is a powerful and active being, which sways the activities of the beings on its surface. It was natural, therefore, in primitive times, to worship this being ; in respect of which, at first, no distinction was or could be drawn as to whether it was alive or merely active ; for the only possible opinion men at that time could form was that, as in their own case, activity was the effect of a set of particular propensities.

This worship of the Earth is found at the outset of all civilizations. We see clear traces of it in the fragments that remain to us of Greek theology :—" This Earth, mother of all men, protectress of all beings, " this common mother."

Language has retained a host of expressions which bring to mind this primitive worship. There is too, a moral disposition, as real as it is world-wide, essentially fetishistic, which is the result of this habit of regarding the Earth as sacred ; and that is the love of one's native soil ; that love which makes us fond of the very place we live in, and binds us to it by a deep attachment. This is unquestionably a fetishistic feeling, and it is well we should follow it ; for, under suitable direction, it may became a source of high moral, and even of intellectual, power. That fondness we feel for certain spots, for sites and remains ; our proneness to invest them with fancies and feelings akin to our own ; these

are fetishistic proclivities, and furnish very clear proof of our deep-seated
tendency to look upon the earth as not merely active—for that it
very evidently is, in spite of the hallucination of metaphysicians to the
contrary—but also as living, animated by sentiment and by will, in
moral relation with ourselves. Hence, the worship of the Earth amongst
the Chinese is bound up with a deep love of the native soil. I may add
that the fetishistic conception of the Sky has not been confined to the
Chinese. Like the adoration of the Earth, it has left its unmistakable
traces in the Western languages.

The proofs of this reduction to a system, in China, of fetishistic
worship, by the adoration of the Sky and of the Earth, are so abundant
that our only difficulty is in choosing which to quote. At Peking, for
instance, amongst nine great altars in the open air we find—taking them
in the order of their importance—altar of the Sky, altar of the Earth,
altar of prayer for obtaining the fruits of the Earth in abundance ; altar
of the rising Sun, altar of the Moon at night, etc.

In all parts of China we find altars dedicated to the Sky and to the
Earth. That is the foundation of the state cult, the official religion.
Other cults are tolerated ; but that is the officially established state
worship. There are, besides those, altars dedicated to the Planets, to the
Constellations, to the various modes of activity of the Earth, to rivers,
etc., etc. Fetishistic worship is, then, the official cult, regularly
organised by the State. At certain epochs of the year, fixed by the rites,
especially at the solstices and the equinoxes, the Emperor, the mandarins, perform official acts of worship to the Sky, to the Earth, etc., etc.,
in the places dedicated to such use. The grand sacrifice to the Sky is
made by the Emperor himself, in an extremely solemn manner, at the
epoch of the winter solstice. The agricultural labour performed by the
Emperor himself has for its special object the raising of the grain
necessary for the performance of the grand sacrifice. We read in the
Li-Ki : " It is for the (sacrifice to the Sky) that the Emperor himself
" does labour in the *Kiao* of the South ; it is in order to offer the grains
" that they are gathered." Besides special temples, peculiar to each
locality, the Capitals or chief-towns of each province, each department
and each canton are officially required to have the following temples :—
altar to the Earth ; altar dedicated to the winds ; to the clouds ; to thunder ;

to rain; to the mountains and to the rivers; an altar dedicated to the first tiller of the soil; a temple dedicated to literature; a temple to the succession of Emperors who have governed China; a temple to the constellation of the Great-Bear; a temple dedicated to the moats which surround and defend the city; a temple dedicated to the evil spirit who causes sickness; an honorary temple dedicated to celebrated statesmen who have done good service to their country; an honorary temple dedicated to country sages; an honorary temple dedicated to men who were models of fidelity, of sincerity, of righteousness and of filial piety; an honorary temple dedicated to maidens who were distinguished for eminent chastity; to married women who were renowned for their virtues and modesty. Such is the official religion. Nevertheless there are, in China, besides temples sacred to the official cult, an immense number of monasteries and religious edifices belonging to the Taoists and Buddhists.—It is evident, then, that Chinese civilization has, for its mental basis, Fetishism, systematised by the worship of the Sky and of the Earth.

As this proposition is of the first importance, and requires to be set forth with all possible distinctness, a few indirect considerations which throw light on it may here be stated. I have already told you how highly developed amongst the Chinese is that essentially fetishistic feeling—love of the natal soil. But, more than that, they have a disposition not less characteristic in this respect, namely, a deep love of nature. This habit of mind, contradictory as it is to the theological spirit in any form, and more especially to monotheism, is highly developed amongst the Chinese; a fact entirely in keeping with the fundamental preponderance which Fetishism has maintained amongst this population. On this point there are proofs in abundance. I shall confine myself to quoting a few lines from M. d'Hervey-Saint-Denys, who has most felicitously and clearly brought out the fact :—

"We," says M. d'Hervey-Saint-Denys, "like flowers; the Chinese "fall in love with them. What pleases us in a garden is the variety of "the view, the richness of the colours, the beauty or variety of the "several kinds of flowers; for the Chinese, each plant is the object of a "veritable cult, of a sort of mystic love, which of itself largely inspires "a great part of their poetic effusions. In their romances, in their

" histories, even in the tenor of their private life, we find instances
" of this simple and passionate love. Grave magistrates invite each
" other to come and admire their peonies and chrysanthemums. It
" even goes so far, in the monuments of Chinese literature, as to seem a
" sort of ecstasy, which our ways do not allow of our being able to
" understand, and which consists in being carried away by the sight of
" the plants while trying to realize, by prolonged attention, the progress
" of their development."

This statement of M. d'Hervey-Saint-Denys is incontestable. In
an interesting moral romance, the translation of which we owe to M.
Abel Remusat, *Iu-kiao-li* or *The Two Cousins*, this love of flowers, of
nature, as a familiar trait of every day life, comes out in the most
unconscious way. There we see too, the happy and affectionate cast of
character which results from this keeping up of the fetishistic spirit. In
fact this attachment for the outer world, for flowers and so forth,
exercises a profoundly softening influence upon Chinese manners : of
that there is no doubt. This moral disposition is again quickening in
the West in proportion as Theologism declines : The theological spirit
hindered it, but could not destroy it.

Lastly, this preponderance of Fetishism, systematised by the worship of the Sky and the Earth, shows itself in another way in the habits
of Chinese life, by the well-known theory of lucky and unlucky days ; a
fetishistic theory of which numerous traces still exist amongst ourselves.

To sum up, then, this long demonstration, we may lay down this
leading proposition :

Chinese civilization has its mental foundation in Fetishism, systematised by the worship of the Sky, whose will, preponderating and
steady, governs all other existences.

It now concerns us to study the consequences, intellectual and
moral, of the civilization that rests upon such a basis.

A necessary consequence of this predominance of Fetishism is that
concrete observation has been greatly developed. Hence comes extreme
acuteness, precision, and we may even say minute exactness, in the
observation of beings. These characteristics are shown in all their
scientific productions; consisting, as those works always essentially do,
of descriptions, and not of abstract theories analogous to those of Western

B

Europe. This spirit of observation, again, shows itself in their paint-
ings of plants and flowers, so remarkable for their extreme stamp of
reality.

A second characteristic, necessarily resulting from the general spirit
of this civilization, is the absence of myths in the systems of the Chinese
thinkers. In all the populations amongst whom Theologism prevails, we
find the legislators, and even the philosophers, making more or less use
of supernatural interventions, and that not so much intentionally as
spontaneously, under the influence of the social environment which
sways them. There is nothing of that sort amongst the Chinese ; and the
fact is one which has struck the judicious observers who have studied
this civilization, though they were unable to trace the phenomenon to
its true source. Neither Confucius nor Mencius nor their successors had
recourse to those supernatural influences so common amongst the
theological populations. They take no account of such arbitrary influences
as gods and genii ; they observe beings, lay down the conditions of
their evolution, and explain them by the influence of other visible and
real beings.

But I must now call attention to the fact that this mental state, in
which abstraction has not been systematically instituted, has produced
in Chinese civilization a double defect; neither science, properly so
called, nor high art have been able to develop themselves within it.

Science is, of necessity, abstract. Science consists, virtually, in
discovering the laws of the various distinct phenomena, geometrical,
physical, chemical, biological, considered in themselves, apart from the
bodies which manifest them. Real science, that which alone admits of
the discovery of genuine laws, necessarily implies abstraction.

It is the same with art. High art is unknown to Chinese civilization ; for, eminent, lofty art rests upon idealization. Now all idealization
implies abstraction, whereby we can leave out some of the circumstances,
and can exaggerate or minify the properties of beings, considered apart
and separately. Idealization can never result from concrete observation,
or the mere observation of beings ; for such observation never transcends
the narrow limits of reality. It is by abstraction—but by real abstraction—that we can conceive types which are truly ideal and yet possible.
Therefore, neither grand creations of science nor grand esthetic creations

could emanate from this civilization. Several observers have been struck by this singular phenomeon, but the explanation of the fact was beyond them, for want of a general theory.

Hence, in China, reality is the striking characteristic of literary works. There are romances of manners and theatrical pieces, remarkable for their naïve portrayal of real life. But grand ideal works, after the manner of Homer and of Dante, have never existed amongst them.

Their scientific development is quite elementary. What science they have comes to them chiefly from the Hindoos, Mussulmans, and Christians; with the exception of that outline which always results from a first spontaneous evolution of the positive spirit.

The deep-seated imperfection, then, which inevitably results from the mental basis of Chinese civilization is the impossibility of a great scientific and esthetic development.

From the moral point of view, the persistence of Fetishism in China has developed the sentiment of fatality and of order, concurrently with a disposition to submission; not, indeed, absolute submission, but relative; of a kind closely approximate to the spirit of scientific subordination.

Observation of beings, especially when, as in the case of the heavenly bodies, it has advanced so far as to have ascertained their regular courses, develops, of necessity, the sentiments of subordination and of order; theological abstraction, on the other hand, institutes the notion of progress, but of a progress which is at first unregulated. Men submit themselves to the external order represented by the regular wills of the preponderant fetishes; but this submission, the foundation of all morality, is by no means absolute; for the correlative beings have only a limited power. This will be better understood if we compare, upon this point, Fetishism with Theologism.

In China, neither rulers nor subjects have experienced the influence, in many respects demoralizing, of the type of a divine being with absolute free-will.

What is, in fact, the type of Deity? It is the freedom to do as pleases himself. An all-powerful being can only have caprices. Genuine devotedness, like wisdom, always implies a certain degree of submissiveness.

" As flies to wanton boys, are we to the gods,
" They kill us for their sport."
                              —*Shakespeare,—" King Lear."*

An all-powerful being may impose obligations ; but these obligations are, on his part, mere whims, founded on no reason beyond his
own will. Such a type as that must, in the long run, have exercised a
more or less demoralizing influence upon both rulers and subjects.
Upon ;rulers, by inciting them to imitate this type of arbitrariness.
Supreme power consisting in the absence of limits upon the acts of will,
surely the supreme happiness of man must consist in the absence of
limits upon the fancies ?   Have not attentive observers remarked the
profound selfishness developed by their all-powerful ;position in those
rulers who, in theocracies, were regarded as consecrated beings ?

But this influence shows itself also in the subjects, acting in the
same way ; impelling them to aim, for their type of happiness, not at an
active and orderly submission, but at a situation which would allow the
the fullest working out of their fancies. In another direction, theologism
tends to develop in subjects obedience of a dull, sodden sort, simply because
it is absolute obedience, and consists in submitting to caprices merely
by reason of their emanating from a superior. This, on the other hand,
gives a profoundly anarchical tone to independence; which then assumes
the aspect of a revolt.   It is the wisdom of the various theological
clergies that has redressed, as far as practicable, the drawbacks inherent
in their doctrines.

China has escaped the moral inconveniences of such a type precisely
because the beings which form the basis of her cult are not gods, but
fetishes ; that is to say, real beings, having a power that is very great,
but not absolute ; a power, too, that is regulated, as we see in the
habitual march of the heavenly bodies.   The happy effects of this persistence of Fetishism can be proven. Amongst the Chinese, submission,
really positive, leads neither to the cringing nor to the unruliness produced by Theologism. This is, perhaps, one of the most important, as it
is amongst the least noticed, of the influences of the Fetishism that dominates this civilization.

Most observers have regarded the Chinese as a people subjected to
an arbitrary despotism, likening their regime in this respect to the

government of Islam in its decrepitude. That is a serious error. A profound submissiveness is, with them, combined with a feeling of very real independence. Chinese philosophers have always maintained that the emperors governed by virtue of a mandate from the Sky; a mandate which could be recalled; and the recall of which was clearly shown by a prolonged continuance of bad government: and the whole history of China, the succession of numerous dynasties, sufficiently shows that this theory was no empty formula.

The king of Ts'i, enquiring of Mencius about events which had happened at dates which even then were ancient, spoke to him of the last prince of the first dynasty, dethroned by Ch'êng T'ang, and of the last prince of the second dynasty, put to death by Wu Wang, founder of the third.

" Are these things true ?" asked he of Mencius.

" History assures us of them," was the reply.

" A subject to put his sovereign to death ! Is that possible ?" replied the prince.

" The rebel," rejoined Mencius, " is he who outrages Humanity. " The brigand is he who revolts against justice. The rebel, the brigand, " is merely an individual. I have heard it said that punishment had, in " the person of Chow, fallen upon an individual. I do not see that in " him a prince was made to perish."

The revolutionary spirit of the West is prone to confound voluntary submission, emanating from real veneration, with absolute submission. The type of human dignity does not consist, as those teachers think it does, in not submitting to anything else than force.

The Chinese, spontaneously, we may say, approximate to the type of true wisdom ; for they feel and understand that true wisdom, active, speculative or moral, is founded upon submission, as the preliminary condition of a well regulated activity. Compare, in this respect, the results of scientific evolution, whose only aim is to reproduce reality by submitting to it, with the puerile metaphysic which aims at constructing it à priori. Such are the unperceived moral effects which the persistence of Fetishism has produced in this great population.

Having considered the influence, upon intelligence and upon feeling, of the mental basis of Chinese civilization, we must now study its action upon the Family, and lastly upon Society, always keeping, of course, the most general point of view.

The Family, the essential element of all society, becomes established and consolidated during the age of Fetishism. But our business now is to see what effect the systematization and persistence of Fetishism in China have had upon the constitution of the Family there,—what special characteristic have they impressed upon it.

We owe to Fetishism the institution of the tomb—that admirable prerogative of the human species, as Vico has finely called it—and the establishment of the worship of ghosts, of the worship of ancestors. This worship of ancestors, so profoundly developed amongst a lettered people who have no belief whatsoever in a future life, was a matter of astonishment to the Jesuits; a sort of paradoxical phenomenon, of which they were utterly unable to find the key. We must dwell for a while on this important notion, so little understood by reason of the persistence' even in the best minds, of the theologico-metaphysical spirit.

Fetishism spontaneously originates *manes ;* a leading notion which lived on during the domination of theologism, especially during polytheism, and which the social wisdom of Roman civilization knew how worthily to uphold.

For the fetishist, all bodies are not merely spontaneously active, but, more than that, endowed with will, passions and feelings. There- fore, for him, death is not what it is for the theologist, the passage to an inert state ; it is the passage from one mode of vitality to another mode. The corpse of one whom we have loved is not, as it is for the theologist, an object of horror, or at least of repulsion ; it is a living being, but living in another way ; having still its inclinations and its feelings, and still taking an interest in wordly affairs. This enables us at once to understand that respect for the remains of the human body is a necessary result of the fetishistic stage of thought. This corpse is still the man you loved and venerated. He has not lost his life, as the theological mind supposes ; he has only taken on another form of vitality. You still owe to him those sentiments of affection you showed him during his first form of existence. The Earth is conceived, by the fetishist, in spite of its apparent immobility, as susceptible of being loved and adored ; why should it not be the same, and for a still stronger reason, with that body you have seen acting in the same way as yourself, and living with your own liveliness ?

The institution, therefore, of the tomb, and the establishment of the worship of the dead result, as neccessary consequences, from the fetishistic stage of human reason.

You see also, Gentlemen, how there follows from this primitive theory the non-belief in a future life. For the fetishist, there is no other world but this one. Upon this Earth alone are we susceptible of two modes of existence ; one with, the other without, locomotion. In both cases there is feeling, affection ; in both we interest ourselves in real affairs. In the second case, we have the mode of vital existence proper to the inorganic bodies which are around us ; only, we must then have a more special affection for those whom we have already loved. The worship of the dead is, then, in natural correlation with the non-belief in a future life. What seemed paradoxical to theological minds is, on the contrary, a thing perfectly natural. Moreover, we find, in the West, that, in proportion as the belief in a future life fades, the worship of the tomb flourishes ; the more a country is under the sway of the theological spirit, the more is the cult of the tomb neglected ; the greater is the repulsion inspired by the remains of mortality. On this point Paris furnishes a proof not to be gainsaid. This Capital of the Emancipation,—is it not the city in which the cult of the tomb is most rapidly gaining ground ?

Worship of the dead, then, has become a leading, essential element in the Chinese Family. Its main characteristic is the worship of ancestors. We always find in every house, when complete, a place consecrated to the tablets of the ancestors. Every ordinary Chinese house has its domestic temple ; a sacred spot, where offerings are periodically made to the ancestors : who are there told of all the important events that take place in the bosom of the family, deaths, marriages, etc. etc. Hence, as a consequence of this grand and admirable institution, respect for age, filial obedience and veneration have attained in China an unusual development. This worship of ancestors, this respect for the *manes*, deeply rooted in their ways of life, is accompanied by an extraordinary degree of attention bestowed upon the coffin. A man gives

himself as much concern about the making of his coffin as about any of
the most essential appurtenances of his existence : it is a matter of the
highest moment. As a consequence of this conception of the *manes*, we
may notice the horror the Chinese have of mutilation ; beheading is a
dreaded mode of execution, because it mutilates. There are curious
traces of this feeling in their novels.

The worship, then, of ancestors, respect for age, filial obedience and
veneration are thus the general characteristics which the mental basis of
Chinese civilization has developed in the family, in a way that should
win the respectful admiration of Occidentals instead of their stupid scorn.

We now proceed to enquire what has been the influence of the
fetishistic spirit upon Chinese Society in general.

The prominent feature of Chinese Society is the absence both of the
institution of castes and of the caste spirit. In China, there are not
only no castes, like those of India, but there is not even an hereditary
aristocracy. The imperial family is not a royal caste, in reality ; though
even if it were, that unique exception, justified by important social considerations, would not at all affect the general scope of our proposition.

The imperial function is hereditary, but not in an absolute way.
The Emperor makes choice, in his own family, of the member of it who
is most worthy to succeed him ; and most frequently it is not the eldest
son who is chosen,—a fact quite at variance with the caste spirit. The
necessarily hereditary character of the supreme function is thus reduced
to its simplest expression, and is in no way an outcome of the spirit of
caste. The Emperor is conceived as governing in virtue of a mandate
of the Sky, which makes him responsible not merely for social disturbances, but for cosmological disturbances also; and the persistent
continuance of a state of disorder is regarded as the decisive token of the
necessity of transmitting the supreme function to another family. We
may say, then, that there never was a population to whom the sway
and the spirit of caste are so utterly foreign as they are to the people
of China. It is beyond doubt that Fetishism is not adapted to produce
the regime of caste. Fetishism, adoring real beings, cannot supply that
absolute consecration which emanates naturally from supernatural
beings. Theologism, on the contrary, spontaneously gives rise to castes,
by sanctioning, in an absolute way, the natural heredity of functions.

During the polytheistic epoch, the regime of caste arises from the fact that individuals of the higher classes can be deemed to be descendants of the gods themselves. Of that condition of mind we have a good illustration in Homer. Monotheism gives to this consecration of the upper classes a still more absolute character, and a greater degree of concentration, in keeping with its more systematic spirit. Hence arises the type of rulers who are not responsible, except before God, and who act because such is their will or good pleasure; a type towards which, under the influence of monotheism, the kingly dictatorship in the West was tending; but the tendency was happily combatted by the military spirit on the one hand, and, on the other, by the gradual evolution of industry and science. Caste attains its complete organization whenever a theological priesthood gains and maintains the upper hand in society; a fact which clearly shows the natural aptitude of the theological spirit for engendering it.

Such is the reason why the grand civilization of China has remained a stranger to caste. In this respect a parallel may be instituted between what China has been and what the West is on the high road to become.

The West is tending more and more to get rid of caste, under the double impulsion of the scientific spirit, and of industrial activity. Hitherto, indeed, the revolutionary spirit has been the sole systematic organ of this general tendency; and the consequence is that it has been forced to assume too absolute a form, leading to anarchy. Caste consists in an *absolute consecration* of the natural tendency of the social functions, private or public, to become hereditary. This tendency receiving an absolute, instead of a relative, consecration, the result, as regards theory, is that merit does not receive its rightful recognition. But, although Western civilization is gradually eliminating this absolute consecration, or spirit of caste, we should not go so far as to take no notice of the real and important bias on which it is founded. Only the Positive spirit can substitute a relative for an absolute consecration, by giving its due share to a natural tendency. Be that as it may, the Western movement toward the gradual elimination of the spirit of caste is spontaneously bringing us closer to the civilization of China, in which caste never appeared.

The absence of caste amongst the Chinese has given them a strong

feeling of independence, and, as a consequence, great personal activity and
enterprise. Hence, amongst this people, an intense, unheard of industrial
activity: insomuch that Auguste Comte regarded them as, pre-eminently,
the active race of mankind. Hence, also, amongst them, a perfect
respect for private property, which forms one of the foundations upon
which their civilization rests. The theoretic notion that the soil belongs
to the supreme authority finds no favour there. Their philosophers
have had a profound feeling that private property is an all-important
basis of moralization. "That is why an enlightened prince, in suitably
dealing with the private property of the people, obtains, for necessary
" result, that, in the first place, children have wherewith to serve their
" father and mother; that in the second place, fathers have wherewith
" to support their wives and children * * * . In such straits, the
" people think only of escaping death; or, fearing to be in want of the
" necessaries of life, how would they have time to trouble themselves
" about moral doctrines, about behaving according to the principles of
" equality and liberty?" (Mencius).

No doubt, there have been there, as in every other social organism,
inevitable disturbances; but we may assert that individual property, the
freedom of transmission, has been respected; and that is an assured
consequence of the absence of castes, and of the independence natural to
minds accustomed to submit only to powers which were capable of being
discussed, at least in principle.

Let us now see what is the governmental type of this society.
Government, the absolutely essential condition of all society, receives a
special character from the theory which consecrates it; although no
theory hitherto has been able, owing to inevitable deficiencies, to
represent all the elements that enter into the constitution of the directing
powers which have arisen in the various human societies. In China, the
governmental type is borrowed from the Family. Not only is the Family
the essential basis of that society, as indeed it is of all others, but the
Government is constructed on the type of the Family. It is not
necessary to believe that this is a necessary incident of every civilization.
It only belongs to fetishistic populations to take, as in the patriarchal
stage, for the type of Government, a generalization of the type of the
Family. What, in fact, is the Emperor, according to Chinese thinkers?

He is the father and the mother of all his subjects. The paternal character is his essential character. The governmental type of theological societies has not been borrowed from the Family, but from the Godhead. The Chinese type has an incontestable moral superiority over the theological type. According to the theological conception, Government has an authority which, in some respects, is outside the pale of discussion : that authority is conceived as, in its essence, more or less capricious and arbitrary. The Deity may subject it to particular conditions of exercise ; but these conditions always seem, at bottom, to be caprices. In real fact, this seeming absolutism is, of necessity, limited by the corresponding sociological environment. When the kings of France assigned their own good pleasure as the final source of their decisions, it was none the less a fact that there were limits which they could not safely have overstepped, and which, indeed, they would never have so much as dreamt of infringing. Nevertheless, their power being conceived as absolute, it was erratically employed, and diverted to acts of arbitrariness such as would never be thought of by one who regarded himself as the father of a great social family, towards whom it was his duty to behave as a father towards his children. This notion has had a profound influence for good on the civilization of China throughout the whole course of its development. Many of the Emperors, in fact, were admirable and touching exemplars of paternal devotedness and firmness of character.

From this conception there results a general disposition of the happiest kind—a disposition on the part of the government, whatever may have been its origin,—even were it military—to push on the development of industrial life ; a tendency otherwise quite in keeping with the spirit of this civilization, but which, in this case, the action of the governmental power consolidates instead of thwarting. It does so by reason of its paternal character. The tendency of the government in China to promote the pacific and industrial bent of the population is thus accounted for.

To sum up ; it follows, from the foregoing difficult abstract estimate, that Chinese civilization has for its mental base Fetishism systematized by the worship of the Sky. Hence results, as the essential element of the society, the family, constituted by filial respect, the paternal power and the worship of ancestors.   Hence, also, comes a fundamental tendency towards a purely pacific regime, and a population free from caste, whose conception of governmental power is moulded upon the type of paternal authority.

OF THE ELEMENTS WHICH HAVE MODIFIED THE CIVILIZATION OF CHINA.

(Philosophy of Lao-tsze.—Buddhism.—Catholicism.)

Having formed an estimate of the general spirit of Chinese civilization, and traced the leading consequences arising therefrom, we have now to study, in a summary way, the elements which have tended to modify it.

Chinese society has, in fact, been in contact, during the course of its development, with other societies which were more or less advanced in the military and theological stage; and it could not but happen that such contact should react upon and, to some extent, modify it.   The Chinese are by no means animated by that feeling of hatred towards foreigners commonly attributed to them.   They are on their guard always against Westerns ; and therein they are quite right.   One cannot but commend their wisdom in that respect; for hitherto they have had no occasion to regard them as anything more than veritable barbarians, pursuing gold and profit by any and every possible means.   But the Chinese have been in contact with peoples of far greater benefit to them than Westerns; and from such contact have resulted the two elements which have exercised the most important modifying influence upon their civilization, namely, the philosophy of Lao-tsze and Buddhism.   Westerns, however, have, in a secondary degree, through Catholicism, and especially through the great mission of the Jesuits, introduced a third modifying element, in all respects the least important of the three.

Broadly speaking, this influence of modifying elements drawn from outside theological sources has been more troublesome than useful to the Chinese.   One result, useful in a secondary sort of way, there has been, no doubt, in the introduction of scientific notions borrowed from Buddhism and Catholicism; but these notions have wrought very little change in the fundamental spirit of Chinese civilization; and, on the other hand, they have been accompanied by such serious moral and intellectual ravages that, to use the energetic language of a Chinese philosopher on this topic, it would have been better for the country if it had never been visited with such a pestilence as the impudent theological spirit which gave rise to them. Be that as it may, what we have now to do is to ascertain, historically, the existence of these three modifying elements, and to form an approximate estimate of what their influence has been.

The first modifying element of Chinese civilization is the philosophy of Lao-tsze, whose followers, widely spread over China, have taken the name of Tao-shi, or followers of Reason.

Lao-tsze was born 604 B. C. (54 years before Confucius), in the kingdom of Tsu, (now the provinces of Hu-peh and Hu-nan), near the Blue river. It is between the Blue river and the Yellow river, and North of the Yellow river, that the grand central germ of Chinese civilization was formed.

Let us first see in what the philosoply of Lao-tsze consists.

It consists in a metaphysical system having for its object to deduce everything from one supreme principle, *Reason*, and to explain everything by abstract properties; so that, like all metaphysics, it ends by presenting mere verbal combinations as if they were real scientific explanations. Such notions have no more genuine value than those of the Neo-Platonists, for example; and I merely mention them for the sake of historical completeness and to show of what sort they were.

" Before the chaos which preceded the birth of heaven and earth," says Lao-tsze, " a single being existed, immense and silent; immov-
" able and always acting but never altering. It may be regarded as the
" mother of the universe. I know not its name, but I designate it by
" the term Reason (Tao). Reason is the inmost essence of all things. It
" has neither beginning nor end. The universe has an end, but this
" Reason has not. Unchangeable before the birth of the universe, it was
" nameless, and ever-existing. Reason is the only name the holy man
" can give it; he also calls it spirit, because there is no place in which it
" is, and no place in which it is not; he calls it *truth*, because there is
" nothing false in it; *principle*, by way of contrast to what is produced or
" secondary. This being is truly *one*. It sustains heaven and earth;
" and in itself has no qualities cognizable by the senses. It is *pure* as
" regards its substance; it is *reason* in respect of the order which it has
" established; it is *nature* in relation to the force which it has given to

" man and which is in him ; it is spirit as to its mode of action without
" bound, without end, etc., etc."—(*Abel Remusat, Posthumous Miscellanies
on Oriental history and literature*)[1].

There we find ourselves in the presence of a full-blown metaphysical
system ; that is to say, of a general explanation by means of indeterminate and arbitrary abstractions.   Metaphysics, properly so
called, always starts with the theological type of thought, rendering it
gradually more and more abstract, so that at last it retains, for its basis
of all explanation, only a general notion of force, one and indeterminate.
It is an essentially diseased stage of human reason, showing the abuse
of abstraction, when abstraction is thus wholly severed from a scientific
basis.   It is a mental state as destitute of intellectual as of social
usefulness.

The leading feature of this philosophy of Lao-tsze is its contempt for
the past, for antecedents ; a feature profoundly opposed to the very
spirit of Chinese civilization.   Contrary to the practice of Confucius, he
never quotes the ancients.

The second characteristic of this philosophy is that it is metaphysical
and abstract, contrary to the concrete spirit of Chinese civilization.

Whence comes Lao-tsze ?   Evidently his origin is foreign.   Probably
his philosophy is a Hindoo importation ; though we have no direct docu-
mentary proofs of such a filiation.   M. Abel Remusat at first upheld the
opinion that Lao-tsze's philosophy was of foreign origin.   He abandoned
that view, however, and latterly maintained that such a philosophy was
the primitive base, the starting point, of Chinese civilization.   This notion,
profoundly irrational, betrays a misunderstanding of the elementary laws
of the working of the intellect.   It is a sheer impossiblity for the intelligence to start with such metaphysical abstractions.   But the irrationality
of the notion is shown still more clearly by a direct analysis of Lao-tsze's
philosophy itself.   So little Chinese is it, in fact, that it fails to recognize
what are precisely the two main characteristics of that civilization,
namely, its respect for the past,—for antecedents, and the preponderance

---

[1] For further details about this metaphysical school, see Abel Remusat,
Melanges posthumes ; G. Pauthier, *Chine Moderne ;* Stanislaus Julien, translation
of the Taoteh King.

of the concrete spirit. Again, so little was this doctrine in accord with its surrounding circumstances that its followers very soon completely degenerated, becoming mere jugglers, magicians, vending the elixir of life. This significant contrast would certainly have engaged the attention of so sagacious and sober a mind as that of M. Abel Remusat were it not that he had undergone a sort of metaphysical bewitchment. At the time when that eminent sinologue was writing, a metaphysic, nowadays discredited, was shining with an ephemeral brilliancy. M. Abel Remusat involuntarily allowed himself to be drawn into representing as the basis of Chinese civilization a doctrine altogether analogous to that which was being upheld in France by *the doctors in insoluble questions,* amidst the plaudits of the literary men of the West. In the main, Lao-tsze, under the impulsion of contact with Hindooism, made an attempt, honorable in itself, to introduce abstraction and abstract theories into China. This attempt was bound to fail, being of a purely metaphysical character, with no corresponding scientific development to rest upon; consequently those abstractions rapidly degenerated into arbitrary wanderings, similar to those we have presented to us in the shameful mental spectacle of the Alexandrian school of thought. Lao-tsze's disciples pursued these abstract ramblings in the midst of an uncongenial environment, and soon degenerated into a sect of magicians and jugglers who now, by means of a theology as worthless from the social as from the mental point of view, make their appeal to the lowest sides of human nature. Hence the followers of Reason, the Taoists, are numerous, often consulted, and nevertheless despised. Often the same spectacle meets us in the West, when unworthy charlatans momentarily seduce public opinion by working upon the fear of death. The Taoists are widely spread over China; though less so than the Buddhists. They have, however, a great number of monasteries.

It remains to be noted that this doctrine was protected by the revolutionary Ts'in She-hwang-ti, of whom more presently. Such a conjunction was the necessary consequence of that contempt for the past, for antecedents, which characterizes the followers of Lao-tsze.

Such is the first of the modificatory elements of Chinese civilization; one which introduced subordinate theological ingredients amongst a population profoundly fetishistic.

The second element which has modified the civilization of China is Buddhism : superior, perhaps, to the doctrine of the followers of Lao-tsze, it has nevertheless exercised an essentially perturbing influence.

Buddhism was introduced into China under the Han dynasty, 65 years before Christ. It is very widely spread all over China. It was fostered by a good many Emperors. All the Chinese are, after a fashion, influenced by it, but in a purely secondary way. Buddhism is in general despised by the literati, the class which represents the true tendencies of Chinese civilization. The Buddhists have organized a cult altogether analogous to the Catholic cult. Analogy of doctrine has produced analogous effects, for there has certainly been no reciprocal communication between the two systems. They have a monastic life completely organized, litanies, relics, etc., etc.

Buddhism has brought serious disadvantages in its train by introducing into China the spirit of theologism, with all the misguided speculative tendencies inherent therein; and these aberrations have been all the more extreme in that Buddhism, properly so called, has no interior hierarchic coördination, like that of Catholicism ; a coördination which has so often served to remedy the disadvantages inherent in its doctrine.

Nevertheless, this element of disturbance has not been productive of such far-reaching deviations as might have been anticipated. Fetishism had been so deeply interfused in Chinese society, this Fetishism had so thoroughly attached the population to the worship of ancestors, of the Sky, of the Earth, at the time when Buddhism made its appearance, that the latter could do no more than merely modify this wide foundation of the civilization in question. A mandarin, though a Buddhist, will nevertheless perform the rites of the official worship ; he will by no means give up the family worship. Thus, the illustrious Emperor Kang-hi, so deservedly praised by the Jesuits, was a Buddhist ; but that fact by no means interfered with his performance of the ceremonies of the state cult. Very correct estimates of Buddhism were formed by literati and Emperors who placed themselves at the true stand-point of Chinese civilization. Thus, the Emperor Wu-Tsung, of the Tang dynasty, (died 846 A.D.), wrote, respecting the necessity of restraining the development of Buddhism, the following lines :—(*Abbé Grosier, vol. 5, p. 51.*)

" Under our three famous dynasties there was never any mention " of Buddha ; it was not till the Han and Wei dynasties that this sect " commenced to spread in China and introduced images.   In the two " courts, in all the towns, in the mountains, nothing now but bonzes of " both sexes, artizans ill employed in making images for them.   The " ancients held it as a maxim that if there was a man who did not work, " or a woman who did not busy herself at her silks, somebody in the " state would have to suffer for it. What, then, must be the consequence " nowadays, when an infinite number of bonzes, men and women, live " and dress by the sweat of others, and occupy an infinity of workmen " in building here and there and everywhere and ornamenting, at great " expense, superb edifices ? "

It could not have been better said. That was the preamble of a decree for the suppression of a great number of Buddhist monasteries and convents.

Buddhism, however, introduced into China some knowledge of astronomy and mathematics ; and that is more than could be said for the followers of Lao-tsze. This slight advantage was more than counterbalanced by the immense inconveniences of an arbitrary theological spirit, prone to stray away from reality, and impelling to a monastic life completely devoid of active occupation.

As for Catholicism, the last modifying element of Chinese civilization, it has not had more than a very secondary influence in China. Nevertheless, it introduced, at the period of the great Jesuit mission, some scientific notions which have been of use.   But, I repeat, its influence was of a very slight and altogether secondary sort ; and I merely mention this third modifying influence by way of bringing it to memory.

We have now finished the abstract consideration of Chinese civilization ; and the really difficult survey thus obtained will serve as the foundation for our concrete study of it.   We shall devote next meeting to the theory of the concrete development of Chinese society, from its origin to our own day.

C

SECOND LECTURE.

(THE FIFTEENTH OF THE COURSE.)

FRIDAY, 13 HOMER, 72—10 FEBRUARY, 1860.

THEORY OF THE DEVELOPMENT OF CHINESE CIVILIZATION.

GENTLEMEN,

In our last lecture we were engaged in forming an abstract estimate of Chinese civilization; that is to say, we ascertained what its main features were; features common alike to all classes of the nation, and to all epochs of its long evolutionary history.

We saw that the mental base of this civilization was Fetishism systematized by the worship of the sky; and we then showed by what elements this civilization had been modified; elements derived from the reaction upon China of other societies outside.

From this fundamental basis we then deduced the leading features of the Family and of the Society.

We showed how the Family, founded upon filial respect and the worship of ancestors, was the basis upon which this society, as indeed all other societies for that matter, was consolidated; but in China, to the extent that the government itself was conceived as moulded upon the type of the family, and not upon the type of deity; an all-important distinction with which the leading peculiarities of government in China are bound up. We saw how utterly non-existent in such a society was the regime of caste; indeed, there was not even a royal caste, in spite of the necessary hereditariness of the supreme function: the result being an admirable combination of independence and submissiveness, the obedience being of a filial kind to a rule largely paternal, in place of the absolute obedience and arbitrary rule which it is the tendency of the theological conception of sovereignty to engender.

Such, in very short compass, is the net result of the abstract appreciation of this civilization we accomplished in last lecture; we are now to enter upon the theory of its concrete evolution.

For this society, the essential bases of which we have defined in the abstract, has been developed in actual fact, and that, too, in the midst of certain particular circumstances. It is the principal phases of this concrete evolution that we are now going to study, and we shall deduce from them, as our final result, a systematic conception of China as she is to-day.

But, before I enter upon the theory of this evolution, I must make a short analysis of the two distinct elementary forces, the mutual combination and interaction of which have had most to do with the course of social development to which I am to-day to direct your attention.

These two elementary forces are :—first, an Imperial family, represented by a single individual who is its head ; secondly, a particular class,—I may call it the Learned class—which was not fully constituted until after the time of Confucius, but the beginnings of which were in existence long before. These two forces have had the directing of the gradual development of this civilization, and have themselves been developed along with it.

Let us proceed to consider the first elementary force of Chinese civilization, that which constitutes its means of unity, to wit, a single personage, the Emperor, in whom is centered the general direction of the society. The Emperor always belongs to one particular family ; so that heredity is the foundation for this supreme function of the social organism ; an exception too well justified by considerations of expediency to require much explanation here. But the heredity differs in kind from the absolute heredity of theocracies. The Emperor has the choice of his successor not merely amongst the children of the Empress proper, but also amongst the sons of the legitimate concubines permitted him by Chinese law, so that the supreme succession may fall, in a family habitually numerous, to the one who is really most worthy of it. Theocratic heredity, on the contrary, is of the absolute sort ; the eldest son succeeds, of necessity, to his father ; whereas here the heredity adapts itself to the claims of public order, in such sort as to combine, so far as the circumstances may admit, the natural advantages of heredity with those of choice. The presence of this first elementary force is an unquestionable fact in the whole course of Chinese history ; and from

the epoch of the earliest legends to our own days we see a single
personage, belonging to one particular family, governing China and
choosing his successor amongst his sons.

Amongst the impulses which sway every Emperor of China there
are two of the highest importance, corresponding to two distinct orders
of functions : the military element or impulse on the one hand, and the
pacific, industrial, administrative, in a word the paternal element or
impulse, on the other. These two sorts of impulses are found at work
deep down in every Chinese Emperor, be his origin or his situation what
it may. Let us look first at the military element. Exist it needs must :
any sort of civilization developing itself in contact with other civilizations must have power to defend itself; and, in another way, this
military element is developed by the necessity of repressing struggles
and intestine disturbances; by the requirements, in fact, of public order.
It is clear that for this purpose, more than for any other, power must
be, and is, effectively concentrated in the Emperor's hands. Therefore
the Emperor of China has always maintained, in a greater or less degree,
a military character. This element is, as we see, essential to the constitution of the monocratic power by which China has ever been directed.

But side by side with this military character, necessitated by the
requirements of the situation, we always find a pacific, industrial,
superintending disposition, which emanates from the very nature of the
civilization itself. I have already explained how the type of Chinese
government was borrowed from the family, not from the type of a god
who does as he pleases. Hence, as a Chinese expression indicates, the
Emperor has always been conceived as the *father* and *mother* of his
people ; as representing, in fact, all the aspirations and all the duties
of the heads of a household, the firmness of the one and the tenderness of
the other; a fact due, as we showed before, to the persistence of the
civilization in its Fetishistic stage of development.

The parts played by these two elements of the inward constitution
of the monocratic power have not always been of the same importance.
Sometimes the military element has had the lead, at other times the
pacific, industrial, administrative element. Nevertheless the general tendency of Chinese civilization has been, in the main, to give preponderance
more and more to the industrial and pacific character.

But whence came the first family of the uninterrupted series of the imperial families of China ? The co-ordination of families into a society is evidently always the work of an influential individual, or, more correctly speaking, of an influential family. Social problems are the outcome of situations, that is, of conditions of affairs in general; but the solution of the problems, let vague humanitarian thinkers say what they will, belongs always to an individual organ. Some one individual must have united the primitive hundred families from whom the population of China claims descent,[1] and to unite them he must have imported into their spontaneous Fetishism a certain primary degree of astrolatric systematization. The individual who founded the first group of this civilization by uniting the hundred families must of necessity have been the founder of the first imperial family, by giving his own family the foremost position in the social structure; and thus the first type of the series was furnished.

The origin and composition of the imperial power being thus accounted for, we have next to enquire how it has worked.

In the first place, the imperial power has been an indispensable element of unity, of stability and of order. It was by this concentration and this hereditary transmission that union and order have been successfully maintained. By these means alone could the society have been really founded, all aspirations converging towards a single centre which represented them and kept them together. In the second place, the imperial power, being of a military stamp, became at once the engine of extension and of defence for the whole society. Upon it naturally devolved the duty of warding off attacks from outside, and of gathering in, by a combination of force and of civilizing action, the populations round about; thus giving to Chinese civilization at once its extension and its durability.

Finally, it must be added, the imperial power·has also been a help to internal progress. The eminent emperors of China have always sanctioned and consolidated progress prepared by the labours of predecessors. It was by them that the successive steps of progress have been acknowledged and definitively incorporated.

---

[1] The Chinese call their own population "the hundred families" (Peh-Sing) probably following a tradition which fixed at that number the families whose union formed the nucleus of the nation.

Thus the imperial power has been, in China, the necessary element of unity, of consolidation, of extension, and even of progress for the correlative civilization.

Let us now consider the second of the elementary forces which have had most to do with the destinies of this civilization, the class of the Learned men, or Literati.

We have shown, and the fact is all-important, that the institution of caste was repugnant to the nature of Chinese civilization. But this civilization, of necessity, gave rise to an enlightened, administrative, lettered, cultivated class, upon whom, under the supremacy of the Emperor, the direction of the social functions naturally devolved. The accumulation of capital, by affording the means and leisure for direct intellectual culture, renders the rise of a distinct class inevitable. This class, owing to the absence in China of the theological spirit, was not constituted into a caste. It remained simply an enlightened class, possessed, of course, of influence ; and upon it the administration of China naturally devolved.

This class, in existence from the outset of Chinese civilization, grew with the growth of a population ever more and more industrious ; but it was only under the impulsion of Confucius and his school that it became the Literate or Learned class, and received, as such, its systematic constitution.[1]

Before his time we find ministers, administrators, generals, etc., etc., emerging, not from separate castes, but from the more cultivated part of the population ; but they have no fixed rules, no co-ordinated doctrine to serve as a flag to rally round. It was in Confucius that this class found its doctor, its organizer. I shall accordingly devote a part of our next lecture to a systematic appreciation of the great school of which this eminent philosopher is the founder. What part has the Learned class played in the sum of Chinese civilization ?

This class has been the regular organ of progress, because it was

---

[1] We have, in the Chow Li, or ritual of the Chow dynasty, a complete picture of the administrative organization of China between the twelfth and eighth centuries before our era; and this work, apart from what we learn more directly but briefly from the Shu King, supplies decisive evidence of the existence of a leading class with the general characteristics I have indicated.

able to follow up a course of activity—industrial, scientific, social,—free from the restrictious and rigid limits which it would have been the tendency of a regime of caste to impose.on it. Enduring whilst Chinese dynasties disappeared one after another, it was, at the same time, the organ of true social continuity. Again, it served as a counterpoise to the power of the Emperors, spontaneously limiting that power, diminishing the military element in it, and tending to develop the pacific and industrial element. The Literate class developed in the Emperor the paternal characteristics; it constructed the theoretical type of the paternal ruler, and, in a slow but unremitting way, pushed towards the realization of such a type. Such was the impulsion under which by degrees was shaped an admirable system of general administration. Lastly, this class is the regular organ of public opinion against inevitable occasional excesses on the part of the sovereign power, and thus constitutes a force that modifies the dominant element.

Such, then, are the two forces—the Emperor and the lettered class— that have played the leading part in the evolution of Chinese civilization.

Having thus finished our abstract estimate of the basis of this civilization, and then ascertained the forces by which it has been directed, we now hold in our hands the clue which is to guide us into the theory of this grand sociological phenomenon, so ill understood hitherto in its totality, notwithstanding the many interesting works that have been written dealing with its details.

I must begin by dispelling a very wide-spread error respecting the supposed immobility of Chinese civilization. According to a view of the matter which Western ignorance has almost stereotyped, the Chinese people attained a certain degree of civilization in the most ancient times, and have never got beyond it since. This conception constitute a real mystery; for which those who hold it can not even have recourse to a revelation. For they admit, without any revelation whatever, the sponta- neous advent of a wide-spread civilization—an idea evidently absurd. They cannot, in fact, explain by what mysterious means so highly developed a social state should all of a sudden have made its appearance two thousand years before Jesus Christ and have then remained prefectly stationary since. Some erudite writers, of considerable eminence too, in their anxiety to give as remote a date as possible to this

civilization, have countenanced the conception. They have accepted
as literally true the dream of a primary golden age believed in by the
Chinese literati. These Chinese men of letters, necessarily looking from
an absolute point of view, could not but carry back into the past the
ideal type of their civilization ; for them every new step of progress was
a return towards a sort of primitive age of gold. This was the process
of the absolute spirit for sanctioning necessary innovations without
rupturing continuity ; a logical process which we meet with everywhere,
and which the scientific spirit alone can replace, by virtue of its relative
character. This dream of an age of gold placed at the outset of Chinese
civilization, taken too seriously by respectable writers, has given consistence to the absurd prejudices of Western ignorance. But this
opinion is altogether irrational. Chinese civilization began, as others
did, with a stage of extreme coarseness. Their primitive traditions
represent their first folks as barely having huts to dwell in, living on
herbs and nuts, etc., etc.,—in short, the state we find at the origin of
other societies. Chinese civilization, then, like all the others, started
from a stage altogether lower, and attained, by a long, gradual development, an immense extension, social as well as territorial.

There is, nevertheless, in this civilization taken as a whole, one
grand characteristic which may have given a certain plausibility to the
absurd opinion I have just refuted. It is this. The evolution of
Chinese civilization has consisted simply in the development of the
germs of its primitive organization. But this grand feature, which I
shall bring out with all distinctness, is an admirable title to the respect
of every true philosopher, not a sign of inferiority, as Western anarchy
supposes.

A noble spectacle truly, which only the normal state will be able to
realize for all societies, is this of the prolonged development of a civilization keeping always the same character throughout, instead of the
changes, more or less sudden and more or less heterogeneous, which the
successive phases of Western civilization present to us. What we see
in the West, starting from the theocratic stage, is that succession of
unlike though inter-connected social states which constituted the Greek,
the Roman, and the Catholic-feudal evolutions : not one of which could
be decently fair to the one that preceded it, and habitually, indeed, could

only curse it. The revolutionary development that began in the four-teenth century has, in many respects, made this bad mental state worse. A series of sudden changes succeeded one another; that we see: the real link by which they were actually bound together has not been seen at all. Western men of letters have generalized such a view of things; they have taken the type of disease for the type of health; and they have adopted this strange conception as their standard for all other civilizations. In China, as a matter of fact, we find nothing at all like these changes of the West. It is always the same civilization, an astrolatric civilization, taking on a continuous increase, but keeping always the same character; a civilization in which contemporaries bless their ancestors instead of stupidly making it their greatness to curse them and misunderstand them. That is the consoling spectacle which China affords us; we see there a truly organic development, in which unceasing progress never ignores continuity, the supreme characteristic of all sociability.

If, in China, we observe a continuous succession in evolution, that does not mean that there have been no revolutions, if, by revolution, we mean only a change of dynasty, not a change in the character of the civilization itself. In the long history of China there have, in fact, been many internal commotions. But to what were they due? They arose from the necessity of changing, from time to time, the family who occupied the throne, the directing element, the central force of the society. The loftiness of the station of imperial power, had notwith-standing the bounds naturally placed on it by opinion and the corpora-tion of the literati, a strong tendency to unsettle, at the end of a certain time, the understanding and the morality of the natures not sufficiently eminent upon whom the supreme function of state oc-casionally devolved. Hence, internal disturbances were the result of dynastic changes that had become necessary. Now such changes are no light matter. The problem is, in fact, to replace the fundamental organ; that which maintains the unity of the whole of the population, and is most intimately bound up with all their ways. Such changes are therefore attended by rude shocks; but these shocks in no way alter the fundamental character of the civilization. It is a matter of eliminating an organ which has fulfilled its function in the social structure. An analogous process normally takes place in individual organisms, with the accompaniment of a pathological disturbance which soon passes away. Such revolutions do not ignore social continuity. The prevalent conception of progress in the West is as absurd as it is immoral. The state of disease, so far from being deplored, is hallowed : development without rule or limit is regarded as a truly normal state. This sad pathological disposition explains how it came to pass that the organic and normal development of a great civilization has been taken as a sign of inferiority by intelligences blunted by the anarchic spirit; a spirit which exercises its spell even over those who think themselves most conservative.

If we look at Chinese civilization as a whole we find, in a sufficiently authentic way, that it extends from the year 2500 before Christ to our own day. Too much importance need not be given to the number 2500 ; but it is always logically useful, especially in sociological enquiries, and when dealing with primitive epochs, to employ figures. They tend to restrain the propensity to rambling vagueness. But their scientific importance for primordial epochs is not so great as for epochs nearer to our own, considering how slow social evolution is at its beginnings. This great civilization, then, has had a period of development extending over more than 4000 years.

The history of the Chinese evolution is divided into two distinct periods. The first extends from about 2500 B. C. till 200 B. C., the time of Ts'in She Hwang-ti. This is the period of foundation. It is separated from the second period by the remarkable reign of Ts'in She Hwang-ti, who was a statesman of puissant energy and strongly marked individuality. He it was who founded the Chinese empire, properly so called.

The second period extends from the year 200 B. C. to our own day. This is the period of development. The Chinese empire, finally constituted, thenceforth presents to us a continuous evolution, the systematic study of which will at length leads us to an estimate of the present condition of that great country.

The first phase is that of the establishing of Chinese civilization, from the beginning till Confucius' time.

This civilization commences with all the attributes by which we have seen it to be distinguished :—Fetishism systematized by worship of the sky; the absence of castes; the existence of an upper class, administering and governing under the direction of a single head; lastly, the family founded on the worship of ancestors and filial respect. Confucius, about 500 B. C., constructs the philosophy which systematizes such a civilization, and thus lays the foundations of a regular organization of the lettered class. This phase is terminated by the energetic military action of Ts'in She Hwang-ti, who at length constitutes China an empire. From this point Chinese civilization, definitively founded, develops itself in a gradual and continuous course.

Chinese philosophers and historians, swayed by a laudable feeling of continuity, have sought to impart to the history of their society a unity which is not possible in the nature of things. They have imagined that the whole of their later civilization existed in the highest antiquity. These are but dreams of a golden age ; what of truth there is in them amounts to no more than this, that the germs of this civilization unquestionably date back to a very ancient time ; but they were merely germs, which only the course of ages could develop.

Tradition places the cradle of Chinese civilization on the banks of the Hwang Ho, or Yellow river, towards the Northern part of its course ; that is to say, towards the provinces of Shen-si and Shan-si. At this spot was formed the group which was to become, by a gradual extension, the Chinese empire.

Chinese civilization next descends that great river, extends itself over both banks, radiates North and South, and at last ends by attaining its present immense extension. Tradition represents the first group as occupying very narrow limits; the current belief being that it was formed of one hundred families, from whom the whole Chinese population claims descent. But apart from that belief, the tradition is compatible with the known laws of formation of all societies. Moreover, this nucleus is described as being at first in a state of downright savagery. But, once formed, bound together by an astrolatric cult, by the systematic worship of the sky introduced by some one influential family, this nucleus, I say, began to act upon the surrounding population in two different ways ; by conquest, and by the natural action of a more advanced civilization upon peoples not yet politically organized, and therefore

little capable of withstanding such an influence. We then see this
society acquiring a firmer constitution and still further extending its
action. But the bent of its primitive energy not being military, the
conquests were not stable; and instead of forming a single empire, formed
around the predominant people a number of groups or distinct kingdoms,
which submitted to the influence of its civilization, but owned no
real political subordination. Chinese historians, wishing to make out a
perfect unity in the development of their civilization, have represented
this state of things as being a sort of breaking up into fragments of a
single empire. Up till the time of Confucius, then, the main phenomenon
that meets us is this :—the development of an astrolatric civilization of
the character before described; the formation of a great number of small
states imbued with that civilization.

We must now enquire what, in such a situation, was the special
rôle of Confucius. Further on, I shall have to discuss this question more
exhaustively; but it is needful here, in order to mark distinctly the steps
of this long evolution, to state now succinctly what his work was.

The task performed by Confucius was that of constructing for the
enlightened, administrative class,—themselves the most notable product
of Chinese civilization,—a philosophic doctrine in which the very nature
of that civilization itself received its systematic expression.

It was a stupendous task; and never, perhaps, has there been a
man who exercised a greater, more profound, more regular action in the
development of any society. The doctrine of Confucius, as we shall see
further on, established the ideal type of the civilization in view. This
systematic doctrine, giving shape to the type to be aimed at, furnished
the ideal around which the theoricians, the administrators, all those, in
a word, who formed part of the enlightened class, were enabled and
impelled to rally. It was the doctrine, in fact, that gave to the class a
constitution, a real unity; it finally founded the class of literati : it is
from Confucius that that class dates its embodiment. From this point
onwards, Chinese civilization develops with the highest intensity and
regularity, because it has acquired, for the first time, a co-ordination of its
second directing element. The first fundamental force, the element of
unity, of consolidation, that is to say, the imperial power, must have
been established from the beginning ; but the modifying element, though

perceptible from the beginning of the society and necessarily part of it, did not attain its co-ordination until after Confucius. The reason is not far to seek. It was of the very essence of the first element that it should be concentrated; it was bound to be systematic, more or less, from the beginning; but the second or modifying element, in its nature dispersive, could only at a later stage attain to the acquisition of the doctrine which gave it co-ordination and enabled it to exercise its characteristic action more effectively.

From Confucius to Ts'in She Hwang-ti (550 B.C. to 221 B.C.) what state of affairs do we see ?

The political situation of China, disunited as it was, remains the same; but the civilization gradually progresses. The literate class acquires, in each of the petty governments, a daily increasing importance. We see the literates going and coming to and fro, taking from kingdom to kingdom their counsels and knowledge of affairs. A philosopher of the sect of Confucius, born in one kingdom, becomes a mandarin, a minister in another. Thus relations more and more regular are established by the literate class between kingdoms politically distinct; in so much that the way becomes gradually prepared for the political unity achieved by Ts'in She Hwang-ti. Similarity of manners and customs is promoted by the influence of the literate class, who are no less active in encouraging the industrial and pacific development of the several peoples amongst whom they move. We thus come to Ts'in She Hwang-ti (221—209 B.C.). Let us note the part played by this great man, and the surpassing importance of his impulsion, notwithstanding the serious mistakes he made.

He belonged by origin to the dynasty of the Ts'in, whose seat was in the North of China, in what is now the province of Shen-si; and he was head of one of the eight dynasties under which the population of China was at that time distributed. He succeeded in conquering all the other kingdoms, uniting the several states under one rule; and thus became the real founder of the Chinese empire. His own kingdom being near neighbour to the Tartars, it was natural that military power should be more carefully cultivated there than in the kingdoms near the mouth of the Yellow river, where a pacific activity prevailed. It is therefore no matter for surprise that the work of conquest fell to his dynasty. His achievement consisted in reducing under one political sway kingdoms which were already allied to one another by a nearly identical civilization. The Chinese empire once really consituted, the conqueror extended his power beyond the Yang-tse-Kiang or Blue river, as far as Tonquin, in the region which is now southern China. He thus gathered into the empire populations which were not really Chinese; amongst whom the civilization before described had not been known. But after their conquest by the arms of the Ts'in monarch these populations were again further subjugated by the civilization of China. At times these two parts of China have seemed to be in antag-onism; but in the sequel there has always been a return to political unity. Therefore this warrior's conquest was, after all that can be said, decisive as regards the consolidation and extension of the Chinese empire.

She Hwang-ti also drove back the Tartars and held them in check. There was an unceasing struggle waged between Chinese civilization, constantly developing and ever enlarging its area, and the nomads who hung upon its borders to the north and west. Ts'in She Hwang-ti defeated them and was fairly successful in keeping them off. He it was who built the famous wall intended to defend China against the Tartars. But this vast structure was rather a monument of vain glory than an efficacious means of defence. In spite of the famous wall, China has been twice conquered by the Mongols and the Manchus. But their conquest amounted, as has been well observed, to little more than the right of mounting guard within the interior of the vast territory. She Hwang-ti largely strengthered the military element in the Chinese Government; hence the strong opposition he encountered from the literati. This military movement, however, was of use, in that it largely aided the firm settlement of the empire of China; but the literati class was too strongly cemented together, and had its roots too deep in the foundations of this civilization for this step of She Hwang-ti's to be anything more than a military dictatorship, temporarily useful toward the laying of a sufficiently firm basis for so large an empire. This mighty task, it must be said, She Hwang-ti accomplished in an extremely violent way. It has often been attempted to justify such violent methods by the pretext of necessity. Such attempts are but an example of that exaggeration to which the absolute spirit is prone. Violence of that sort is ever the outcome of moral inferiority in natures in many other respects eminent. The literati, imbued with the feeling of continuity, anxious for the administration, for the paternal character which it was their aim to maintain in the government of China, wholly failed to understand how useful, how necessary She Hwang-ti's policy was for really laying the foundations of Chinese empire and giving it a sufficient reserve of stability against attacks from without. They could not sufficiently free their minds from the ancient type ; and they confronted the monarch and his minister Li-sze with a keen and persistent opposition. Their resistance then prompted him to a measure of extreme and brutal violence. He ordered all books to be destroyed, especially the ancient books, most venerated by the people ; and forbade, under pain of death, any one to keep a copy of them. This barbarous order was carried out with the utmost cruelty. Though its complete success was, in the nature of things, impossible, it called forth admirable displays of devotedness on the part of the literati. They showed a noble courage in defending those books in which the wisdom of preceding ages was condensed. Such was the extreme, the unjustifiable measure of the new ruler, who thus, with unpardonable violence, broke down an opposition very natural in itself, and which, in so far as it was unreasonable, he might easily have overcome without recourse to such savage expedients. Be it noted, however, that Ts'in She Hwang-ti, so bitterly hostile to the literate class, the followers of Confucius, was, on the other hand, a declared partizan of the followers of reason, the Taoists. And the reason is plain. The Taoists, like all metaphysicians whatever, had more or less, a contempt for the past; they were sure to be in sympathy with a revolutionary like the Ts'in conqueror. Confucius's followers, on the contrary, true representatives that they were of Chinese civilization, had the profoundest respect for antiquity. Indeed, it is worth noticing, that when favour is accorded by Chinese emperors to Taoists or Buddhists, it is generally a sign of retrogression ; a fact easily understood when we consider the inferiority of those two systems of doctrine, with their proclivity to vague mental aberrance.

Such is the summary analysis of this first phase of Chinese civilization.

That civilization has, in all its essentials, been founded; the Chinese empire has at length been established. It may experience shocks, struggles, dismemberments; but the different elements will always draw together again by virtue of their previous association and by the influence of the literate class more and more systematically organized. We shall now turn to the second phase in the continuous development of this civilization, henceforth firmly set upon its foundations.

From 200 B. C. to our own day the history of China shows us a great number of dynasties, some of which reigned simultaneously, during periods of anarchy. But as our concern here is not with a detailed, concrete history of China, but with a systematic survey of the general march of its civilization, we shall notice, in this long period, only six great dynasties—the Han, the Tang, the Sung, the Yuen or Mongols, the Ming, and the Ta Tsing or dynasty of the Manchus. These dynasties are separated by intervals of anarchy, or even of political decomposition; but it is worthy of note that these intervals of anarchy go on diminishing in duration and intensity in proportion as the civilization consolidates and spreads. The dates of the six principal dynasties are as follows :—

First the Han, from 202 before Christ till 263 after Christ; then follows the Tang, from 618 till 905; the Sung, from 960 till 1119; the Yuen or Mongols, from 1295 till 1341; the Ming, from 1368 till 1573; the Manchus, or Ta Tsing (great pure) dynasty from 1618 to the present day.

This brief list gives us great chronological landmarks, of which we shall take advantage to set forth, in intervals of time not arbitrarily chosen, the successive steps of progress made by the society we are studying: between the Han and the Tang we see a real political break-up of China; as likewise between the Tang and the Yuen. Nevertheless, during the time of the dynasties that then reigned simultaneously, the progress of Chinese civilization was not stopped; it only moved more slowly; the stamp of unity deeply imprinted by Ts'in She Hwang-ti, and the fundamental similarity of manners and beliefs, systematically represented by the literati class, availed, after the lapse of a certain time, to restore to political unity a civilization ever more and more homogeneous.

Two kinds of progress went on during this long period; the internal development of Chinese society, and secondly, its territorial extension. Consequently, its resistance against the surrounding populations (Tartars, Thibetans,) became more efficacious than ever, and ended by bringing them under control; so that China had all needful stability before she came into contact with the West. This double movement of inward action and outward reaction now claims our attention.

We notice that an important industrial discovery, indispensable to the development of the literati class, was made in the time of the Ts'in despot and improved upon subsequently; namely, the invention of paper and ink. The improvement of the pencil, or writing brush, is attributed to Meng Tien, the most eminent of She Hwang-ti's generals. It is not at all uncommon, in China, for important industrial improvements to be made by military men. So writing with the brush and ink upon paper superseded graving upon bamboo slips, which was the usual mode of propagating documents previously, though on rare occasions inscriptions were engraved on stone. Graving upon slips of bamboo was a tedious and troublesome process, suited only to an early stage of development of the theoretic and administrative class. As soon as that class began to enlarge along with the expansion of an increasingly industrial society, there was a natural straining after some better means of transcribing speech. The invention of paper and ink was therefore brought about in a natural way by the wants of the time. This step of progress, once achieved, was of immense help to the development of the learned administrative class, by facilitating the propagation and acquisition of information; and by thus augmenting the number of well-informed people it of course still further aided the progress of the civilization they moved in. The invention steadily spread, from the time of Ts'in She Hwang-ti and the great Han dynasty; and the manufacture of paper became one of the important industries of China.

The second emperor of the Han dynasty, Hwei Ti, (the Benevolent Emperor, 194 to 187 B.C.), revoked Ts'in She Hwang-ti's decree against the ancient books, thus remedying the element of oppression and violence with which that innovator had carried out his reforms. The Han dynasty thus aimed at the work of repair; it walked in the approved

D

way of Chinese civilization and developed it, while preserving what was
essential in Ts'in She Hwang-ti's work, the political unity and a better
administrative centralization.   One of the best types of the Han dynasty
was Wên Ti (179 to 156 B.C.).   He encouraged letters, promoted the
improvement of agriculture, and in a truly paternal spirit governed with
firmness and energy.   He realized that noble moral type of the highest
function which Confucius and his school had sketched.

Thus, with reference to an eclipse,—a phenomenon of high importance
in China, owing to the astrolatric basis of the national worship,—Wên
Ti published a truly characteristic declaration :—

"I have always heard that Heaven gives to the people it produces
"superiors to nourish and govern them.   When these superiors, masters
"of other men, are without virtue and govern badly, Heaven, to make them
"enter the path of duty, sends, or threatens them with, calamities.   In
"this eleventh month there has been an eclipse of the sun.   What a
"a warning that is to me ! On high, the stars lose their light; below, our
"people are in misery.   I recognize in all this my deficiency of virtue.
"Immediately on the publication of this declaration, let there be an inves-
"tigation with all possible attention throughout the whole empire as to
"what my faults are, in order that I may be warned of them.   To this end
"let the most enlightened, righteous and firm persons be sought for and
"presented to me; on my part, I recommend all those who are in charge
"to apply themselves more closely than ever to fulfilling their duties, and
"in particular, to retrench all useless expenditure, that the people may
"profit thereby."

Here we see arising, under the initiative of Wên Ti, the regular
right of memorializing the emperor, a capital step of progress in this
monocratic government.   This right of presenting memorials, openly
proclaimed by Wên Ti and ever since maintained, was afterwards
developed and co-ordinated by the institution of a Council of Censors,
whose duty is to warn the emperor.   This function, the exercise of which
has often been dangerous, has afforded scope for instances of admirable
devotedness on the part of the literati, and put a check upon the
arbitrariness which supreme power tends to beget.   We see in this
institution of the Censorate a characteristic example of the continuous
effort made by the literate class to exercise a moderating action upon the

imperial power, by the regular impact of public opinion. For the observations of the Censors, published in the Imperial Gazette, are reproduced by the gazettes of the provinces.

In like manner, Wên Ti repealed, by an express declaration, the law of T'sin She Hwang-ti which forbade criticism of the government :—

" To-day We find amongst our laws one which makes it a crime to " speak evil of the government ; the effect of this is not only to deprive " us of the lights which We might receive from the wisdom of those who " are far away from us, but also to shut the mouths of the officers of our " Court. How, then, is the Prince henceforth to be informed of his " faults and shortcomings ? This law, moreover, leads to another " mischief; under pretext that the people have made solemn public " profession of fidelity, submission and respect towards the Prince, if " any one seems in the smallest matter to fail to make good his profes- " sion, he is accused of rebellion. The most indifferent remarks are set " down, when it pleases the magistrates, as seditious murmurs against " the government. Thus the people, simple and ignorant, find, without " thinking of it, that they are accused of a capital offence. No ; We " cannot endure it; let that law be repealed."

On this edict the Emperor Kang Hi made the following remarkable comment : " Ts'in She Hwang-ti had made many such laws. Most of " them were repealed by the founder of the Han dynasty. This par- "ticular law was not repealed till the time of his successor Wên Ti. " That was too long to wait."

One of the successors of Wên Ti was Wu Ti, (the Warrior Emperor, 140 to 86 B.C.), who not only promoted the internal development of China, but exerted a vigorous and successful reaction upon the surrounding barbarous populations ; thus making an initial step in that process of extension which, terminating in the eighteenth century, was destined to add Tartary and Thibet, as subordinate constituents, to the great oriental empire. Under Wên Ti the study of history in China was strenuously cultivated. It was in this reign that Sze-ma Ts'ien (the Herodotus of China) compiled his great work the "Historical Records," which is in fact a cyclopedia. (See M. Abel Remusat's notice of it in his *New Asiatic Miscellanies*, Vol. II).

It was under this dynasty that Buddhism, officially introduced into

China, acquired there an importance which has since too often been baleful; though under the present dynasty it has proved a useful political instrument for dealing with the peoples of Tartary and Thibet, who are under the sway of the Buddhistic creed.

Between the dynasty of the Han and that of the Tang (from 268 to 618 B. C.) a long period intervened, marked often by anarchy, and throughout by political dispersion, the consequence of the convulsions attendant on the necessary displacement of the Han dynasty.

The Tang dynasty, extending over the period from 618 to 905 A. D., is one of the most noteworthy in Chinese history. It is the literary dynasty. It witnessed the appearance of a vast number of literary productions, romances and dramas. Under this dynasty one grand step of progress was accomplished, the establishment of the system of examinations for office.

This was an event of no slight importance ; for it was the means by which the literati class were put in the way of attaining that organization which they still preserve. The learned class had developed enormously. From it were taken the ministers of state, the administrators, the judges,—all those in short whose calling it was to direct that industrious population. The need of having guarantees in choosing men for administrative posts, so as to render their action as a class uniform, must have made itself felt. It was, then, the essential needs of such a state of affairs that brought about the establishment of the system of examinations. Once established, this system profoundly consolidated the class in question, by giving it more of unity, and therefore more force. Thenceforward it was no longer a vague and ill-defined class, from which the emperor might choose or he might not. It was a really co-ordinated class, wherein the examinations undergone were the legal stepping stone whereby gradual promotion to the highest functions of state was to be attained. This step of progress, giving to the literati greater consistence as a class, had the result of improving its action upon the whole mass of the civilization. The evolution of the society was thereby continued on the same general lines as before. Under this dynasty, too, public schools, colleges, education generally, and the Confucian cult were more and more extended.

One of the most eminent types of the Tang was Tai Tsung (627 to

649 after Christ). In him we recognize that ideal of an emperor which was outlined by Confucius and elaborated by his school. " He ordained " that from that time forth Chinese Emperors, before confirming sentence "of death passed upon criminals, should fast for three days." The punishment of death is sanctioned only by the Emperor, except in cases of necessary immediate repression. This definitive confirmation of sentences of death takes place at a fixed period of the year ; and we see with what noble moral precautions the Emperor Tai Tsung surrounded the solemn act by which the necessary elimination of a member of society is authorized. We are here evidently far away from that mere arbitrariness of a theocracy which has been so lightly attributed to such a government as that of China.

Tai Tsung forwarded the development of filial piety, the basis of the family and ultimately of society. He organized a vast system of public works ; also assistance for the aged and infirm ; and his successors continued that aid. The establishment also of foundling hospitals shows how absurd are the tirades upon which Western ignorance is fed as regards the alleged regular organization of infanticide. He wrote a work on the art of reigning.

" After I have given," says he, " each day the necessary time to " transacting affairs of state, I make it my pleasure to project my view " and thoughts over the histories of the past ; I examine what were " the manners of each dynasty, the good and bad examples of all the " princes, the revolutions and their causes. I always do so with " advantage ; and I have done it so much that I can talk upon the " subject."

His recommendations to his children are admirable.

" My son, be just, but be good ; reign over yourself, have absolute " sway over your passions and you shall reign without difficulty over " the hearts of your subjects. Your good example, far more than your " most rigorous orders, will make them fulfil all their duties with " exactitude. Punish seldom and with moderation ; but scatter benefits " with full hands : never put off till the morrow a favour which you can " confer the same day ; postpone, on the other hand, chastisement " until you have assured yourself that it is deserved."

It is under this dynasty that the famous Chinese Academy, the

Han-lin, was established ; a body composed of the most intelligent and cultivated minds, and which has an important share in the literary, political, and moral direction of China.

This puissant dynasty made its power felt over the Turks and Tartars as far as the Caspian sea.

It was about the year 931, under the later Tang emperors, that the art of printing was invented in China by the Minister Fung Tao. Movable types are not used ; merely graving on wood. The whole book is engraved on wooden blocks, and then printed, for the most part in a very economical style. Such an invention was strongly called for by the nature and the requirements of the civilization ; and there is room for surprise that it should have had to wait such a long interval after the invention of paper and ink, its indispensable preliminaries. The need of plentifully multiplying copies in a country where the literate class was largely increasing, must have pushed forward the discovery of some way of printing that would admit of copies of the various works being easily and rapidly produced. The situation called for the invention ; and it is not surprising that such an invention should at length have been made amongst so highly industrious a people. The printing is not our mode of printing with movable types ; it consists of wooden blocks or plates, on which are carved in relief the characters forming the work to be reproduced. In the eleventh century of our era the Chinese did, indeed, advance to the invention of movable types ; but they make little use of them, preferring the impressions from engraved plates ; not out of the spirit of mere adherence to routine, as Western fatuity supposes, but for very sound reasons.

There are two reasons why the Chinese have made very little use of movable types for printing, one of them being a social reason, consequent on the conditions of their civilization, the other consequent on the nature of their system of writing.

The social reason is that the Chinese are much given to reprinting the same books. In the revolutionary West the abuse prevails of producing mediocre, inferior books garbled from excellent original works. China, to be sure, produces commentaries in plenty ; but the respect for social continuity leads to the reprinting of the same texts over and over again. The wooden blocks are therefore worth keeping, all the more so as they can be easily and cheaply touched up when they have got worn. It deserves to be noted that publishing can be done in China much more cheaply than in the West. The printing is done on only one side of the sheet, and very rapidly. A workman can strike off two thousand sheets a day.

But there is also another very good reason for the preference of the Chinese for their own mode of printing; and that is the nature of their script. With us elementary sounds are represented by letters, few in number, by combinations of which all words can be reproduced. Hence our use of movable letter types. Not so in China. Their writing is not phonetic; or rather, more accurately speaking, their characters do not represent the elementary sounds, few in number, of which all words whatsoever are made up. When a Chinese written sign or character is used in a phonetic way, it expresses a whole word, not a single articulation merely; and this phonetic sign is rarely employed alone; it is usually joined to an ideographic sign, in combination with it. Hence their characters are extremely numerous, and are susceptible of being increased idefinitely, so as to keep pace with the progress of their civilization. The number of these characters may be placed as high as thirty thousand at least. From that it may be seen what an immense number of them it would be necessary to make. The Chinese therefore felt no want of movable type for printing; and when the art was discovered, they naturally preferred printing from engraved plates, as really the more convenient and economical method of the two.[1]

In the wake of the invention of printing came the institution of Gazettes; at first the Imperial Gazette, and ultimately provincial Gazettes, by means of which communication is easily and rapidly established between the government and the people. Besides these, the practice of posting up placards, so useful for making appeal to public opinion, is employed both by the government and the public.

Under the Sung dynasty (960 to 1126 B.C.), the system of examina-

---

[1] Nevertheless, the adoption by the Chinese of movable type printing is merely a question of time. The practical difficulties, thanks to Christian missionary zeal, have been largely overcome. Block printing has, in Japan, been almost entirely superseded already by movable types.—Tr.

tious, already in operation for the civil service, was extended to army
appointments, much in the same way as examinations have to be
undergone in France for admission to the Military, Naval, and Polytechnic
schools.   The only point that seems to call for remark on this subject
is the continual tendency towards the elimination of the arbitrary
element in the monocratic power that presides over the destinies of this
great people.   The attainment of public office is thus not left wholly to
the caprice of a master, but is determined by a regular series of proofs
of fitness given.

The great Yuen or Mongol dynasty governed China for 88 years,
from 1280 to 1368, after its establishment by a conquest which the
Chinese were unable to avert, owing to the political anarchy which the
deposition of a dynasty, when necessary, always entails.

The establishment of the Mongol dynasty supplies us with a
capital illustration of the part played by the corporation of the literati
as the systematic depositaries of the leading intellectual and moral
results of this civilization, and consequently of the character of continuity
which they have stamped upon it, thereby keeping its development
homogeneous.

Thus Yehlü Ts'uts'ai, prime minister of Ogdai, (son and successor
in 1229, of Genghis Khan), though a Tartar, was an eminent literate,
versed at once in all the learning of China and in the profoundest
astronomical knowledge of the Mussulmans.   Besides introducing that
knowledge into China, he led his master to understand how important,
how necessary it was to employ the literati as judges and administrators.   He thereby began, with great tact and devotedness, the work of
incorporating the conquerors into the Chinese civilization, so as to
ensure its continuity and its progress.   " Tartar by origin, and become
" a Chinese by the culture of his mind, he was the natural inter-
" mediary between the oppressed race and their oppressors.   Placed in
" high office near the person of Genghis Khan and his successor, he
" found himself a sort of protecting providence of the conquered people ;
" and his whole life was spent in pleading before the triumphant
" barbarism the cause of the laws, of good order, of civilization and
" humanity.   He substituted the sway of reason for the yoke of force,
" the power of institutions for that of the sword, a system of regular

"imposts for pillage, the slow but irresistible influence of the literati of "China for the coarse authority of the conquering Tartars."—(*Abel Remusat, new Asiatic Miscellanies.*)

The real founder of the Yuen or Mongol dynasty, Kublai Khan (in Chinese Hu-pi-lieh), grandson of Genghis, continued the same policy, and on a grander scale. He became a Chinese himself, and did his utmost to extend his adopted civilization; and this line of conquerors may be accounted as amongst those which have contributed to the greatness of China. It was Kublai who made Peking the capital of the Empire. It was in Kublai's reign, too, that the Mongols introduced Lamaism, a form of Buddhism peculiar to Thibet, and marked by an organization of the clergy such as that religion seldom elsewhere exhibits. Kublai died in 1294; not before he had added several finishing touches to the system of Chinese administration, and a much needed stiffening to the army.

In short, the Mongol dynasty maintained the greatness of the empire, and bore a part in promoting its internal development. When the royal house deteriorated, and increasing incapacity rendered its complete elimination necessary, the Chinese expelled it, and drove out its Mongol followers at the same time; and thus to the Yuen dynasty succeeded the native dynasty of the Ming (1368-1616).

The T'ai Tsu (*great ancestor*, 1327-1398) or first sovereign of the line, chose the dynastic style Ming, which means light. Apart from their dynastic style, it is the custom of Chinese Emperors to give to the years of their reign a name indicative of the qualities by which they desire them to be signalized, and it is this name of the reign-years that Europeans habitually mistake for the name of the Emperor himself. Thus K'ang Hi means *tranquil prosperity;* but it passes amongst us as being the name of the Emperor who chose this phrase as the designation for the years of his reign. The reign-name of the founder of the Ming dynasty was Hung Wu, (wide warfare), and it is by this name that European writers designate that sovereign himself. He was born in 1327 at Sze-chow, a town in the province of Kiang-nan. The son of a labourer, he became a Buddhist monk. In the midst of the struggles which marked the decline of the Mongol dynasty he forsook the cloister, and before long gathered round him a vast number of followers, by whose

prowess he succeeded in expelling the Mongols, and even made some of
their tribes his vassals.   In home affairs he made use of the lettered
class to re-establish order ; and he consolidated, by his expeditions
against the Tartars, the results of the measures which the coöperation of
the literati enabled him to achieve for the further development of the
national civilization.   This great man's policy was continued by his immediate successors.   Hung Wu, following the Chinese usage—a usage
of high social utility—published his last will ; in which he set forth the
reasons for his choice of a successor, and at the same time gave such
instructions as befitted that solemn announcement.   This combination
of a choice freely made within the circle of the imperial family, and of a
public announcement of the choice and of the reasons for it, is a social
institution which, in the coming normal state, human societies will
adopt and practise on a much wider scale.   Hung Wu perfected the
internal administration of his empire, promoted useful public works,
founded plans of relief for the aged and infirm, extended the practice
of the worship of ancestors, of Confucius and of eminent men ; and
in a word, actively displayed during a long career all those genuinely
social traits which characterize the true type of a Chinese emperor.

After shining with great lustre and rendering weighty services
this dynasty of the Mings gradually changed its character, under the
intoxicating influences of supreme power.   In the midst of the struggles
which necessarily followed in the wake of such a degeneration, the
Manchu dynasty, now reigning, came upon the scene as conquerors.
The conquest was only effected after the utmost resistance had been
offered ; but China was in a state of such utter anarchy at the time that
opposition was unavailing.

The present dynasty dates, officially, from 1616.   It has contributed
to the development of China in the most efficacious way ; on the one
hand forwarding, with as much activity as wisdom, its internal development; and, on the other, finally reducing Tartary and Thibet to
tributary subjection; thus giving all needful stability to this great
civilization before the disturbing occasion of its contact with the West.

Previous to its contacts with the West, what, in point of fact, was
the element that caused disturbance to Chinese civilization ?   Evidently
it was the Tartars; that is to say, it was a population, or rather a group-

of populations, nomadic or only half settled in their mode of life, necessarily in continual struggle with this industrial, wealthy and peaceful
society. Various have been the issues of these struggles; the Tartars
often beaten back, and at times vanquished; at other times, victorious;
but in the latter case commingling and incorporating themselves in the
civilization of China, and, after a period of more or less violent oscillation,
helping on its development. The conversion of the Tartars to Buddhism
after Genghis evidently paved the way for the definitive subjugation
effected by the present Manchu dynasty. K'ang Hi and K'ien Lung, the
two leading representatives of this dynasty, at last rendered the Tartars
and Thibetans tributary; thereby giving to Chinese civilization all the
consolidation that was either possible or required.

The best known in Europe of the Emperors of China was K'ang
Hi, contemporary of Louis XIV, (reigned from 1662 till 1723). He
accorded to the great mission of the Jesuits a sage and enlightened
protection. He sagaciously perceived the utility of incorporating with
Chinese civilization the scientific knowledge that had been amassed by
the peoples of the West. He placed a Jesuit at the head of the Board of
Astronomers, after he had, by a judicious experiment, satisfied himself
of the superiority of Western over Chinese astronomy. The experiment
he devised was this: he ordered both parties to calculate, what, on a
given day, would be the length of the shadow cast by a gnomon of a
certain size; a problem which involved a knowledge of the declination of
of the sun on that day, and of the solution of a right-angled triangle. The
forecasts of the Jesuits were confirmed by experience when the day
came, whilst those of the Chinese astronomers were not; a fact which
clearly shows that their astronomy was in a state of infancy. After
having completely re-established order in the interior of his empire and
having, abroad, by a sage combination of policy and war, prevented the
formation of a new Tartar power similar to that of Genghis Khan,
K'ang Hi devoted his long career to promoting the internal well-being
of his vast dominions. Himself a distinguished scholar, he actively
encouraged the spread of letters throughout his realm.

His grandson Kao Tsung Shun, called in Europe by the name of the
years of his reign K'ien Lung, (enduring prosperity), reigned from 1736
to 1796. He completed the subjugation of Tartary, and definitively

secured the submission of Thibet. In Thibet it is apparently the Dalai
Lama who governs, but he is really under control of the Chinese mandarins. Under this great and magnificent Emperor internal changes were
effected in keeping with the importance of his expeditions abroad. He
largely promoted works of public utility, especially certain great operations for preventing the overflowings of the Yellow river. I borrow
from M. Abel Remusat a few sentences in which he characterises the
noble nature of this prince, and that sense of responsibility which led
him to regard the supreme power as a social function imposing
imperative *duties;* a conception completely in accordance with the
philosophy of Confucius, and one which so many worthy Emperors,
under the pressure and with the aid of the body of literati, have
succeeded in practically realizing.

" In proportion as the Emperor advanced in age he became more
" punctilious in his performance of the ceremonies which form part of
" the duties of the sovereign ; and when the infirmities under which he
" suffered obliged him to relax somewhat his exactitude, he justified
" himself by public declarations of the reasons of his inability. He
" was thus all the more diligent in his application to affairs of state ;
" and at the age of ninety he used to rise in the middle of the night in
" the severest season of the year, to give audiences or transact business
" with his ministers.

" He was gifted with a firm character, a penetrating mind, a rare
" activity and a high sense of right. He loved his people as a Chinese
" sovereign ought to love them ; that is to say, he was careful to govern
" them with firmness, and at all costs to maintain peace and plenty
" amongst his subjects. Six times in the course of his reign he visited
" the Southern provinces, and each time it was for the purpose of issuing
" useful orders ; causing dykes to be constructed along the margin of
" the sea, or punishing the malversations of the great officials, towards
" whom he showed himself inflexible."

K'ien Lung actively fostered the development of literature, and the
general diffusion of instruction : he was himself a distinguished scholar.
The missionaries had, therefore, good grounds for putting at the head of
the last of their series of *memoires,* those published by Père Amiot, the
following verse :—

Though ever busied with the cares
That link with rule of vast domains,
The mightiest potentate earth bears
Is scholar best his realm contains.

We have now, Gentlemen, finished our survey,—a cursory one, it is true, but sufficient for our purpose—of the concrete development of this civilization. We have witnessed, as it were, the gradual unfolding of a double phenomenon ; the internal development of an industrial and pacific society, under the combined direction of a monocratic power and of an administrative class recruited by a regular system of examinations from all ranks of the population ; and on the other hand, in the midst of continual struggles, the steady enlargement and expansion of that society, which finally subordinates to itself the outside populations by which it had been frequently disturbed.

Having thus brought our general survey to its close, we must sum up by showing what has been the final outcome of it all ; in other words, we must attempt a summary sketch of the present condition of this great civilization.

The long evolution, Gentlemen, of which I have established the abstract theory and then given a concrete summary, resulted finally in the formation, in the farthest East, of an immense society, the product of a long and unbroken elaboration of four thousand years. It is this final result that we have now briefly to examine and judge of in its entirety. The view of this great society, at once stable and progressive, which has obtained, far better than any other that has ever yet existed, the so much needed conciliation between order and progress, will suffice to convince you of the superficiality of the foolish prejudices which, in the West, give cover to the ignoble sentiments so prevalent upon this subject.

The Chinese empire is composed of China proper and of the countries tributary to it, which are : Thibet, Eastern Turkistan, Zungaria, Mongolia, the country of the Manchus, and Corea, besides a great number of islands off the Eastern shores of China, amongst them Formosa. The subjugation of these tributary countries at the close of the eighteenth century, after struggles that date back to the very infancy of China, and constitute the history of its outward activity, gives to this civilization its essential stability; to say nothing of the service rendered to humanity by its civilizing action upon backward populations whose formidable excursions in times of yore gave so much trouble even to Western Europe.

China proper is comprised between the degrees 20° and 42° of North latitude and of 97° and 122° East longitude ; which makes an extent of 1,500 miles from North to South, and of about 1,200 miles from East to West, or a superficies of over one and a half million square miles. I do not reckon as being in China proper three provinces in the country of Liao-tung and of the Manchus, which were annexed by K'ien Lung, and placed under a different mode of government from that of the tributary states. China proper is divided into eighteen provinces.

Here is a table of the population of these eighteen provinces, as obtained from the returns of the official census of 1852 and that of 1812.

OFFICIAL CENSUS OF 1852 AND 1812.

PROVINCES.	CAPITALS.	POPULATION IN 1812.	POPULATION IN 1852.
1. Chihli	Pao-ting Fu	27,990,871	40,000,000
2. Shantung	Tsinan "	28,958,764	41,700,621
3. Shansi	Taiyuen "	14,004,210	20,166,972
4. Honan	Kaifung "	23,037,171	33,173,526
5. Kiangsu	Kiangning "	37,843,501	54,494,641
6. Nganhwui	Nangking "	34,168,059	49,201,992
7. Kiangsi	Nanchang "	23,046,999	43,814,866
8. Fuhkien	Fuhchow "	14,777,410	22,699,460
9. Chehkiang	Hangchow "	26,256,784	37,809,765
10. Hupeh	Wuchang "	27,370,098	39,412,940
11. Hunan	Changsha "	18,652,207	26,859,608
12. Shensi	Singan "	10,207,256	14,698,499
13. Kansuh	Lanchow "	15,193,125	21,878,190
14. Szech'wan	Chingtu "	21,435,678	30,867,875
15. Kwangtung	Kwangchow "	19,174,030	27,610,128
16. Kwangsi	Kweilin "	7,313,895	10,584,429
17. Yunnan	Yunnan "	5,561,430	8,008,300
18. Kweichow	Kweiyang "	5,288,219	7,615,025
Totals		360,279,597	536,909,300

We may say that China proper has a population of at least 400,000,000 of inhabitants subject to a uniform system of government ; a fact which is surely, in itself, the most striking result of a social evolution of unparalleled duration and continuity.

Let us first of all see what is the general kind of activity mainly and chiefly manifested by this immense population. A grand spectacle we have there before us, Gentlemen ; a population of fully four hundred millions given up to an activity that is essentially pacific and industrial, and amongst whom, thanks to the subjugation of Tartary by the dynasty now ruling, the army is reduced to the normal function of mere police, that of maintaining order against internal disturbance, whether occasioned by individuals or by mobs.

Private property is perfectly respected, alike in the acquisition, the employment and the transmission of it ; and this is as true in the case of movable property as in the holding of land. Security,—in this respect the essential basis of all activity, as of all civilization,—is as great in China as it is in the best governed countries of Western Europe.[1] The land is very much parcelled out ; the system of small properties has there been carried to a high degree of development. The class of small cultivators, the farmers, are held in such respect that they rank next after the literati. Even where large farming exists it is the exception, not the rule. Large farming is essentially modern, and peculiar to the

---

[1] "The great wealth of the empire, the cheerful and indefatigable industry of the people, and their unconquerable attachment to their country, are all of them circumstances which prove, that, if the government is jealous in guarding its rights, it is not altogether ignorant or unmindful of its duties. We are no unqualified admirers of the Chinese system, but would willingly explain, if possible, some of the causes which tend to the production of results whose existence nobody pretends to deny. In practice there is of course a great deal of inevitable abuse; but upon the whole, and with relation to ultimate effects, the machine works well: and we repeat that the surest proofs of this are apparent on the very face of the most cheerfully industrious and orderly, and the most wealthy, nation of Asia. It may be observed that we make great account of the circumstance of *cheerful* industry ; because this characteristic, which is the first to strike all visitors of China, is the best proof in the world that the people possess their full share of the results of their own labour. Men do not toil either willingly or effectively for hard masters."—*The Chinese : by John Francis Davis.*

West. It is a consequence of the development of the abstractive faculty amongst the people of the extreme West. In the future, large farming will be, to a far greater extent than it is at present, the condition and the basis upon which agricultural industry will be systematized. Cattle-grazing, the forerunner of large farming, can hardly be said to exist in China, especially in the South. The culture of cereals, and, above all, of rice, is the great object of Chinese agriculture. The absence of grazing farms, and the consequent scarcity of manure, in spite of the indescribable trouble the Chinese take to utilize everything in that way, is inevitably a cause of exhaustion of the soil. But these undeniable inconveniences, inherent, indeed, in the nature of such a civilization, are far more than compensated by the existence of the immense class of small cultivators; a class free, energetic and independent; traits which necessarily result from the hard-working, sober life of a population whose personal property is respected as it should be.

The culture of pot herbs, of flowers, gardening, has been highly developed in China, and has attained an unrivalled degree of perfection. The culture of trees, as the bamboo, the tea shrub, etc., is one of the great branches of husbandry. The staple of Chinese food is essentially vegetable. Of animal food, pigs and fowls are the main items. In the Northern provinces of China, supplies of beef, mutton and venison are got from Tartary. The implements of husbandry are of the simplest kind. The skill and vigour of the husbandman makes up for the inevitable imperfection of his implements, in keeping, as they are, with the small properties they are used upon. For the rest, Chinese agriculture enjoys the benefit of a vast system of irrigation works. We may therefore readily understand the tremendous importance the Chinese people attach to irregularities in the weather, fraught as these may easily be with such serious consequences for the food supply of so vast a population. Hence the immense development of public granaries, of which we shall make mention again. And this extreme concern about the phenomena of the weather has been greatly accentuated by the fetishism in which the whole civilization is rooted.

Agriculture is the main end of the activity of this pacific population. Public opinion in China has always sanctioned the pre-eminence accorded to this essential basis of all industrial activity.

Let us now take a look at their manufactures and commerce, that is to say, the work of appropriating raw materials and the establishment of means for facilitating exchange of commodities.

Their industrial processes are essentially empirical, and show little or nothing of that employment of machinery which comes of the practical applications of the abstract sciences ; but the Chinese display, in their industries, a remarkable activeness and sagacity, combined with indomitable patience and great sobriety. We should note, what indeed may be readily conceived, that Chinese industry is, above all, petty industry ; that is, on a small scale, just as their husbandry is petty husbandry. This is a consequence of the insufficient concentration of capital, and of their inferiority in the employment of large machines.

The silk industry has, in China, and has had from the highest antiquity, a noteworthy importance and dimensions. In the single city of Hang-chow more than 60,000 workers in silk were counted, and more than 100,000 in the villages adjoining it. The cotton industry in China has a like, but somewhat lesser importance than that of silk. As for the porcelain industry, its perfection and the immense amount of its productions are too well known to require description. But, to convey an idea of the industrial activeness of this population, making use of everything with unflagging perseverance, I may cite the following words, written by a missionary of the seventeenth century (*New Account of China, written by Father Gabriel de Magaillans, of the Society of Jesus*) :—

"For, as in this kingdom there is not a useless foot of land, so " neither is there a man nor woman, young, old, halt, maimed, deaf or " blind, who is without the means of making his living, without an art " or occupation of some sort. The Chinese have a common saying, ' In " the kingdom of China nothing is thrown away.' However worthless " or useless a thing may appear, a use is found for it, a profit of some " sort made out of it. For instance, in the city of Peking alone there are " more than a thousand families whose sole means of livelihood consists " in selling matches or sulphur tipped touch-wood for kindling fires : " there are at least as many more who live by raking up, in the streets " and amongst sweepings, rags of silk stuffs, rags of cotton and hemp

E

" fabrics, bits of paper and other such like things ; which they wash and
" clean up and then sell to others, who put the fragments to use in a
" variety of ways by which they make a profit."

By way of conveying a notion of the industrial sagacity of the
Chinese people I may point out the various services they contrive to get
by cultivating the bamboo.

The Chinese have, by systematic cultivation, attained such skill as
to be able to produce an immense variety of kinds of bamboo : varieties
in size and height, in the distance of the knots, in the colour of the wood,
in the superficies of the stem, in the substance and thickness of the
wood, in the branches, in the leaves; in short, they produce fixed
peculiarities in the bamboo, and these peculiar features are perpetuated ;
such, for instance, as the formation of shoots or fleshy excrescences,
good to eat. The bamboo, thus improved by skilful cultivation, is employed for a host of purposes.

" The young sprouts of bamboo, when they begin to come forth
" from the earth, are as tender and as delicate as asparagus. They are
" cut, and form a wholesome and agreeable article of food. The con-
" sumption of this comestible is immense, and gives rise to a consider-
" able trade. What is not required for local consumption is carried
" elsewhere, even to the furthest ends of the empire. To prevent the
" young sprouts from rotting, they are cut in quarters, then steamed for
" a certain time and dried. Thus prepared, they keep for a long time,
" and can bear transport to great distances. The bamboo, though
" hollow, is very strong, and, used as a pole, can bear very heavy loads ;
" and is occasionally used in place of wood in carpentry. The trunk is
" very hard to cut across, but can be split lengthwise with the greatest
" ease. Sometimes mats are made of the thin threads into which it can
" be divided; and a host of pretty things, such as boxes with com-
" partments, combs, etc., are made from bamboo slips. Being naturally
" hollowed pipes, the bamboo stems are used as conduits for water both
" under and above ground. The stems, when broken fine and macerated
" in water, form a pulp or paste of which different kinds of paper are made.
" The wood of the bamboo, smooth, close and easily polished, admits of
" every kind of ornamental carving, and can be gilt or silvered or em-
" bossed with ivory. Boiled in cabbage water and subjected to pressure,

" it will receive, and keep permanently, impressions all over its surface.
" According to Father Cibot, it is no exaggeration to say that the mines
" of this great empire are of less value to it than its bamboos ; and that
" next to rice and silk, it possesses no greater source of revenue."
(*L'Abbé Grosier, China, vol. II. p. 381.*)

The real commerce of China is its internal commerce, which is
developed on an enormous scale. The amount of this home trade may
be easily imagined when we take into account the immense extent of the
empire and the density of its population. The trade is mainly carried
on by water. China is one vast net work of rivers and canals ; its inland
navigation is tremendous. The government carefully looks after these
channels of inter-communication between the various provinces. China
is a world apart, self-sufficing : it does, in fact, itself supply its own
needs in no inadequate way.

"I navigated," says Father Magaillans, "by order of the Emperor,
" in the year 1656, the whole of the grand canal and other rivers from
" Peking to Macao, more than 1500 miles, without going by land more
" than one day's journey, and that was to cross a mountain which
" separates the province of Kiangsi from that of Kwangtung. On the
" 4th of May, 1642, I set out from the town of Hangchow, capital of
" the province of Chehkiang, and on the 28th of August of the same
" year I arrived at the city of Chingtu, the capital of Sz'ch'uen. In
" those four months I travelled, always by water, more than 1000
" miles, counting the windings of the rivers ; one month of the time I
" navigated two different rivers, but for the other three months I was
" always on the great river Kiang, the child of the ocean, as it is called.
" Throughout that long voyage I daily met such a number of trains or
" rafts of wood of all sorts that if they were all joined together they
" would have made a bridge which it would have taken several days to
" walk over. I sailed by some of them that were moored to the bank by
" the hour at a time, and sometimes for half a day."

This vast home trade has been largely developed since the time
when Father Magaillans wrote. Indeed, the foreign trade of China is
quite insignificant for such a population, in spite of the great impulse
given to it in the present century. Foreign trade has done China more
harm than good, by communicating to her mainly our vices, to say

nothing of the special dangers attendant upon contact with people
who acknowledge no duties of any sort towards Oriental populations.[1]

Again, trade with the West (that with Russia excepted) is not, so
far as China is concerned, an exchange of useful commodities; China
is paid in money. Two thousand years ago an Emperor of China,
placing himself worthily at the social point of view, formed a very
judicious estimate of the worth of trade of that sort :—

"Money that comes into a country by trade only enriches it in so
"far as it again goes out of it by trade. There is no trade that is
"beneficial in the long run but that which consists in necessary or
"useful exchanges. Trade in objects of display, of finery or of fancy,
"whether it be made by way of barter or purchase, implies luxury. Now
"luxury, which means superfluous abundance on the part of certain
"citizens, implies the want of necessaries on the part of many others.
"The more horses rich people harness to their chariots, the more people
"there are who have to go on foot. The more vast and magnificent
"their houses are, the smaller and more miserable are the houses of
"the poor; the more their tables are covered with viands, the more
"people there are who have to live upon rice. The best that we in
"society can do by force of industry, of work and economy, is to secure
"that all have the necessaries and some the comforts of life."

Such, then, Gentlemen, is the general activity of this industrious
population. We have now to study its constitution, estimating first,
the family, and then the society properly so called.

The foundation of the family in China, and indeed, as I have already
shown, of all society, is filial piety, the feeling of respect for father and
mother and ancestors. The family as thus constituted upon its essential
basis, the power of the father, the reverence for ancestors, have been
constant subjects of concern with Chinese legislators and philosophers.

The cult of ancestors and of the tomb, a consequence of the fetishistic spirit, has been reduced to system in China in such a way as to
constitute a private worship which has strongly consolidated the family;
regular visits to the tomb, carefully keeping it in order, are essential duties

---

[1] These strictures were more just a quarter of a century ago than they
are now.—*Tr.*

of every Chinese, whatever be the doctrines, theological, Buddhistic or other, which may have been superadded to the fetishistic substratum of his mental state. Every family, however numerous its branches, has a common hall of ancestors, in which regular commemoration ceremonies are performed, and in these the place of honour is always assigned to age, independent of social station. Again in each branch family a room is set apart for direct ancestors, in which are placed the tablets which represent them, and there the head of the house always goes to inform them of all events of any importance which take place in the family.

Such is the admirable institution of the cult of ancestors; an institution very closely allied to the ideal normal state of the human family, of which the essential characteristic is *continuity*. To develop this sentiment systematically is the best way to assure the true progress of the family, by developing what is most organic in its constitution. This respect for *continuity*, largely developed in the Family, besides ensuring to the family its due stability, serves also to prepare for Society natures truly organic, and free from that disrespect for the past which, in the peoples of the West, stimulates all kinds of disturbances in the present. We may therefore rest assured of the correctness of the Chinese maxim that a bad son is ever a bad citizen. And, to complete the matter, this fine constitution of the family has been perfected in a characteristic way by the admirable social custom which makes the glory acquired by descendants date back to the ancestors, instead of being handed down to the successors, the plan followed in the theocratic regime. So holy an institution will always merit the respect of every true philosopher; and in proportion as, under the impulsion of the religion of Humanity, the West advances towards the normal state, it will incorporate in suitable fashion this grand creation. In place of the Western usage which, in most cases, especially in our times, only ensures to the successor of an eminent man the possibility of an idle and useless life, the Chinese institution, resting upon a fully developed sentiment of filial piety, offers, as the principal recompense for noble efforts, the possibility of bringing honour on one's ancestors, whilst at the same time it encourages the desire of so training up successors that they may be worthy some day so to glorify one's name.

The relations between brothers, far from being left to an anarchical equality, as in the West, are morally regulated on the principle of the younger being subordinate to the elder; and this conduces not only to the order and stability of the family, but also to the development of true brotherly affection. In spite of the superficial prejudice of the revolutionary spirit, it cannot be denied that a certain degree of recognized subordination, creating as it does reciprocal duties, is far more favourable to the engendering of real affection than an unregulated equality, which only serves to foster strife between selfish rivalries and claims.

Finally, the very development of Chinese civilization itself, has, silently and imperceptibly, reacted upon the Family in such a way as to give it further strength and perfectness. Such reaction is due to the influence necessarily exercised upon the Family by the very fact that the Society has had a long course of evolution, of which the continuity has never really been broken. However far back a Chinese may go in tracing the series of his ancestors, he always finds himself in natural sympathy of opinion with them; consequently the respect for ancestors always derives additional strength from consideration of the past, instead of being weakened by it. In the West, on the contrary, the continuity of social evolution has been often broken. How, for example, can respect for ancestors attain, in a Christian, any very deep consistence, when, in tracing far enough back the series of the ages, he comes to ancestors whom he is bound to hold as accursed? A doctrine which establishes itself by cursing its predecessors must exert a sad influence upon the feeling of respect for ancestors. Hence the cult of ancestors and of the tomb, which fetishism bequeathed to polytheism, has been disowned and neglected by monotheism. In Corneille's great master-piece, Pauline, as a pagan, respects her father's orders; as a Christian, she becomes, to follow her own expression,—

"A holy rebel 'gainst the laws of birth."

The revolutionary movement, properly so called, has greatly aggravated the profound moral mischief wrought by the rupture of social continuity. How can filial respect flourish in a society where each generation despises and curses the one which immediately preceded it? In the West, then, the inevitable reaction of the revolutionary state shakes and destroys that sacred foundation of the family which the continuous evolution of Chinese civilization strengthens and consolidates.

In spite of the stupid conceit of revolutionary Christians, deists or atheists, the Family is, in China, so far as regards the filial and fraternal relations, much nearer the normal state than is the Family in the West, and is therefore, in those points, deserving of imitation and respect.

It is in the conjugal relations that the relative inferiority of the Chinese Family is manifested. The monogamic stage of social development has been only imperfectly attained in China. The law only allows one legitimate wife, but it sanctions a regular concubinage. It should be noted, however, that this legal concubinage is, in point of fact, confined to those who are rich, or really well off; and that even amongst these it is far from being as extensively practised as the law would allow. Whereas, in the West, especially in the great centres of activity, we only too often see an irregular concubinage, which binds to no legal duty whatever, take the place of the regular concubinage for which Chinese legislation makes provision. When, however, the West, regenerated, shall be in a position to maintain with China intercourse of a kind other than that growing out of an unbridled rapacity, it will most assuredly be in the amelioration of the conjugal relations amongst the well-to-do classes in China that it will be able to make its beneficent action felt. It is on this point that the Western Family, especially if regenerated by the Demonstrable Faith, shows its true superiority, whilst it is undeniably inferior, in our own days more than ever, as regards the filial and the fraternal relations. And, of a truth, the Chinese can do more for the moral amelioration of the West, by the spectacle they present to us of a regulated society, than we can do for their intellectual and material amelioration by the dubious benefit of our industrial improvements; especially when these improvements are being pushed on with a daily increasing disregard of the moral effects of the changes they produce. This ignoring of the moral and social aspects of industrial progress, has, however loudly an extravagant liberalism may protest, an incontrovertible tendency to produce, as the type of civilized man, a materially very powerful sort of brute. Indeed the consequences of this shameless industrial licentiousness as seen in the labouring classes,—for it is there that the effects of the movement are felt in their fullest intensity,—are not in the least likely to attract the Chinese in the direction of imitation.

Let us now form an estimate of the Society, in the widest acceptation of that term, and first of all, of its cult.

Fetishistic adoration systematized by astrolatry is, as I have shown, the official cult of China. But with this official worship is coupled that of great men, or rather the systematic worship of all those, men or women, who have rendered to society any services whatever, intellectual, industrial or moral. This worship of noble natures is headed by that of Confucius.

After the Sky and Earth, Confucius comes next in importance as an object of worship: he is, for China, pre-eminently The Philosopher, and when we come to form a systematic estimate of that great sage we shall find that he well deserves the worship paid to him. The cult, then, of great and noble natures, completing a fetishistic Sky-worship—such is the official cult of China, faithfully representing the real spirit of that great civilization and giving to that spirit, by means of its regular exercises, a firmer consistency. It is clear that the regular cult of great natures was sure to spring up amongst a people with whom the very constitution of the family had led to the regular cult of ancestors. The cult paid to the family's ancestors was extended to the ancestors of the society. This systematic respect for the past, the mark of a truly organic civilization, kept up and developed that respect for old age which we derive from Fetishism, but which, in common with the other foundations of all sociability, is being more and more compromised by our Western anarchy. We have thus, in the official cult of China, a homogeneous series, combining the adoration of the principal exterior beings (heaven, earth, rivers) with the adoration or cult of the principal representatives of society, from the greatest philosophers down to the direct ancestors of each family.

Provinces remarkable for particular productions have special temples. Thus the province of Chekiang has a temple dedicated to the first silk-worms, because sericulture has been developed in that province from time immemorial.

The mandarins are the priests of the official cult; the solemn sacrifices to the Sky are celebrated by the Emperor in person.

But beside and along with the official cult a Chinaman will make use of religious ceremonies borrowed from Taoism, or Buddhism, or other belief more or less superstitious. Many even of the mandarins do not remain exclusively faithful to the orthodox official cult, but combine with it Buddhist or Taoist practices. But these practices neither in any way alter nor enter into the official cult of China ; they are, in fact, often despised by the very persons who yet make use of them. And a respect for Buddha is a matter of necessity with a government which numbers immense Buddhistic populations amongst its tributaries. But the real statesmen of China have a clear and judicious appreciation of the superiority of the official cult over the theological cults which exist alongside of it. I will quote here a few passages which are conclusive on that point. The Emperor Kang Hi published, under the name of *Sacred Edict*, a number of moral maxims, upon which a commentary was written by order of his successor Yung Ching. A mandarin, Superintendent of the Salt gabelle in Shensi, named Wang Yu-po, wrote a paraphrase of the work which is current throughout the empire ; and it contains some truly characteristic observations on the topic we are now treating of.

One of the points which the royal commentator inculcates with the greatest force is the aversion for false sects ; and that of Fo (Buddha) which is of alien origin, is the object of his special disapproval. He speaks with contempt of the dogmas on which it is founded, and pours derision upon its practices. The Buddhists, like the followers of other Indian sects, attach great importance to certain sacred words or sacred syllables, which they perpetually repeat; believing that by the mere articulation of these holy syllables they purify themselves from all their sins, and ensure their salvation by this easy devotion. The literate treats this usage with amusing raillery. " Suppose," says he, " that you " had committed some violation of the law, and that you were being led " into the judgment-hall to receive sentence ; if you were to take to " crying out with all your might ' Your Worship ' some thousands of " times, do you imagine that the magistrate would let you off for that ? " (*Abel Remusat, Asiatic Miscellanies.*)

The literate then sums up, with great good sense, the demonstration of the inferiority inherent in any theological cult.

" If you neglect to burn paper in honour of Buddha, or to lay " offerings on his altars, he will be displeased with you, and will let his

"judgments fall upon your heads. Your god Buddha, then, is a mean
"fellow. Take for a pattern the magistrate of your district. Even if
"you never go near him to compliment him or pay court to him, so
"long as you are honest folk and attentive to your duty, he will be
"none the less ready to attend to you; but if you transgress the law,
"if you commit violence, or trespass on the rights of others, it would be
"useless for you to try a thousand ways of flattering him : you will
"always be subject to his displeasure."

The same literate, following up the views of the Emperor Yung
Ching, expresses the following judgment of the Catholic religion and the
part it had played in China :—

"The sect of the Lord of the Sky too, (Catholicism), that sect which
"is always discoursing about heaven and earth and about beings without
"shadow or substance, that religion is itself a corrupt and perverted one.
"But, because the Europeans who teach it know astronomy and mathe-
"matics, the government employs them to correct the calendar. That,
"however, does not signify that their religion is a good one ; and you are
"not in any way bound to believe what they tell you. "

Such is the point of view systematically taken by the true literati in
judging of all theological religions whatsoever.

Having gained an insight into the cult, we must now rapidly sketch
the organization of this vast empire.

The government is concentrated in the hands of the Emperor. He
has supreme sway ; but although, in the last resort, every decision
emanates from him, this sway is limited, like all power whatever, by
the mass of opinions and rules established from time immemorial, which
no dynasty could long violate with impunity. As an instance of such
checks, take the fact on which I have already dwelt at some length, that
the imperial type is borrowed from the family ; that the emperor is
regarded, and regards himself, as the father of his subjects, and therefore
bound by the duties of such a function ; not as a sort of divinity, acting
according to arbitrary caprices, after the manner of the theological type.
It is under the constant weight, therefore, of such a conception that the
sovereign sway is exercised and accepted. Besides that, a set of
practices and precepts, long ago created as the sequel of the social
antecedents, regulates the exercise of the sovereign power.

The emperor chooses his successor amongst his children, keeping clear, as much as possible, of those hereditary trammels which are imposed under the regime of theocracies.

There is no hereditary aristocracy. The reason of this grand sociological phenomenon I explained in my previous lecture. The governing class recruits itself, by examinations duly graduated, from amongst all classes of the population. There are three successive examinations conferring degrees corresponding nearly to our Bachelor of Arts, Master of Arts and Doctor. The degree of Bachelor, or Licentiate is open to every one who passes the regular provincial examination. The Masters, in turn, are chosen, by examinations, from amongst the Bachelors; and the Doctors, by the same method, of course, are taken from amongst the Masters. Government employés, even for the highest posts, are chosen out of the Masters and Doctors. So that China is administered and governed by a class that is not hereditary, emanating from the ranks of the people, through a regular system of tests which give merit its due. In practice many abuses may be, and no doubt are, committed in the obtaining of degrees; but taken in the whole as it stands, this organization governs and administers a population of over four hundred millions of men in such a way as to secure for the greatest number material and moral existence as well, certainly, as those benefits are secured for any other population of the planet.

Such, then, Gentlemen, is the governing class; so constituted and so recruited throughout the empire. Let us now see how it regularly distributes and shares the diverse special offices.

At the summit of the hierarchy are placed two Councils, one, the Grand Council, or Council of State, the other the Grand Secretariat. It is the duty of these Councils to look after the whole machinery of the government.

Then come the Six Boards, sitting at Peking, which control, each in its allotted department, the working of the state regulations. They constitute, in fact, the central administration. They are :—

1. The Board of Civil Office, charged with the choosing, appointments and promotion of the civil functionaries of all grades.

2. The Board of Revenue, having charge of all that relates to the taxes, duties and revenue of the empire.

3. The Board of Ceremonies, which has the superintendence of everything connected with rites, the worship of the ancestors of the reigning dynasty, and grand solemnities, civil or religious.

4. The Board of War.

5. The Board of Punishments.

6. The Board of Works.

Each of these Boards is directed by a council, with the President at its head, who has less power than a Minister of State in Europe, as he is under the necessity of consulting his colleagues. Under the present dynasty each Board has two Presidents, respectively Manchu and Chinese.

Each Board, again, is divided into sub-departments. The Board of Revenue, for instance, has fourteen such subordinate branches; whilst the Board of Rites has only four.

Let us now see, Gentlemen, the territorial distribution of the empire. China proper is divided into eighteen provinces. A Governor, or sometimes a Governor General, is placed over each province, though a Governor General has mostly two provinces for his jurisdiction. I have already given the population of each of the provinces, as collated from the census of 1812 and 1852. Some of them are each as populous as France. They are each subdivided into Prefectures, Departments, Districts and Townships, villages or communes. In addition to the Prefects, the Governor of each province has, as subordinates, the Provincial Treasurer, the Provincial Judge, the Salt Comptroller and the Grain Intendant. Under the Prefects, again, are Sub-prefects, Department Magistrates, District Magistrates and smaller mandarins; and, finally, the communes are directed by headmen and municipal councils elected by the people.

I cannot now enter into the full details of this vast system of administration. I can only bestow a passing mention on the organization of public works; on the regularly arranged system of public granaries for remedying the calamities of famine years; on the alms-houses for the aged, and the foundling hospitals established and maintained by joint contributions from the government and private individuals. The existence of the last named institutions is in itself a sufficient reply to the ignoble calumnies current about an alleged systematic organization of infanticide; calumnies that are made use of in order to play upon the silly self-conceit of good people of the West.

To sum up, then, Gentlemen; we see in the Far East an immense population, essentially industrial and pacific; governed, under the preponderance of a monarch, by a class regularly emanating from the ranks of the people through the medium of a well organized system of examinations; and consequently without any hereditary aristocracy. This class of learned men has gradually built up a vast system of administration, under the direction of which are living a population of four hundred millions of men. And this society, after long efforts, has finally brought into association with itself the less advanced populations around it, which had been heretofore a perpetual source of trouble to it; so that it has at length been able to reduce its army to what is destined to be the normal function of all armies, namely, that of a gendarmerie or police.

It is this immense society which the anarchical contacts of the West are tending to trouble and oppress. But before laying down the principles of a truly rational policy for the West to follow with respect thereto, I must first attempt an estimate of Confucius, the most systematic representative of this great civilization.

THIRD LECTURE.

(THE SIXTEENTH OF THE COURSE.)
FRIDAY, 20 HOMER, 72—17 FEBRUARY, 1860.

ESTIMATE OF CONFUCIUS AND OF HIS INFLUENCE ON CHINESE CIVILIZATION.

·GENTLEMEN,

In the last two lectures we briefly estimated, first, the fundamental spirit of Chinese civilization, then the general history of its concrete development, in such a way as to deduce from this double investigation a clear and determinate knowledge of the existing condition of that great empire. We saw the Chinese empire gradually shaping itself by an evolutionary process, the main laws of which I endeavoured to expound. In that philosophical theory of Chinese civilization I briefly referred to the part played in it by its most eminent philosopher, the founder of the essential basis upon which the modificatory element of that civilization was built up. I showed, in fact, that two fundamental elements have concurred in that evolution: an imperial family, exercising a monocratic government, but liable to be superseded in cases of imperious necessity; and an enlightened, learned class, by which the sovereign power is at once modified and regulated.

The man who laid the foundation for the systematic co-ordination of this great class was Confucius. It was needful, therefore, that a special study should be made of that philosopher; but the task will also be useful in another way; it will develop in us that just sentiment of respect which will enable us to see in him the concrete embodiment of the civilization of his race. That is why we are going to devote the first part of this evening's lecture to a special estimate of Confucius's work.

I must first delineate the general situation in the midst of which Confucius arose. We shall thus see under the weight of what antecedents he acted, and how he was the organ of the fundamental necessities of a situation created by the past; we shall then better comprehend the enormous power of his action when we see how suitably adapted it was to the spirit of the civilization in and on which he worked. Confucius, in fact, is one of the men who have most profoundly influenced their social environment.

It has first to be explained how it came to pass that the efforts of Confucius and his school had to be directed to morals, especially practical morals, and to works of erudition, or of concrete sociology.

Chinese civilization is, as we have shown, essentially fetishistic; and it is in that direction that it has been developed. A consequence of of this has been that China has been deprived of the social institution of abstraction. The institution of abstraction is one of the grandest creations of Humanity; and the mental evolution of the advanced populations has been due to its influence. All the high intellects of the West have worked under the impulsion of that great institution. They felt its power without being able to give any account of it; for it is to Auguste Comte that we owe the discovery and the systematization of this grand sociological phenomenon, by the dogmatic and historic contrast which he established between the abstract and the concrete sciences. For social influences, like cosmological, are felt long before high intellects discover their laws.

Theologism brought in abstraction by the special representation of the various distinct phenomena by means of corresponding gods. Now, in China, theologism not having spontaneously arisen, there could be no deep and familiar working of the abstractive faculty. Now, abstraction is the necessary condition of all great scientific elaborations, as of all high esthetic development.

The truth of this, as regards science, is manifest. There is no real science but abstract science. It is only by studying the various distinct phenomena that we can succeed in ascertaining their laws. It was thus that mathematics, physics, chemistry, biology, and finally—by Auguste Comte's grand creation—sociology, were gradually developed in the West. China, consequently, wholly fetishistic as she was, could show no great scientific movement akin to that of the West; nothing even analogous to the intellectual movement of India.

And it is the same as regards great esthetic creations : abstraction is the essential basis of idealization. Idealization is the condition under which alone really high art is possible. Now abstraction idealizes, on the one hand, by the elimination of certain properties, and on the other hand because, by allowing of the properties being considered separately from the beings which manifest them, it then becomes possible to conceive of extreme limits of variation, both more and less. China, rich in artistic productions, of secondary merit as being too exact representations of reality, had to remain a stranger to high esthetic creations, poetic or plastic.

Thus a stranger to theologism, and therefore to the institution of abstraction, China presented an unfavourable medium for the elaborations of pure science, as for the creations of high art.

Such is the explanation of the singular fact, often remarked upon, of a great people having produced immense works of erudition and of moral philosophy, whilst neither science properly so called nor really high art have ever been able so much as to make an appearance amongst them.

Such a general situation as that repels great intellects, of a theoretic cast, from purely abstract speculations or from great artistic creations.

That is one primary general fact which dominates the whole mental evolution of this civilization.

But the social situation, properly so called, tends in the same direction as the intellectual situation by inclining, towards moral speculations, and especially practical morals, the theorizing intellects which the latter repels from works of pure science.

We have shown that one of the leading characteristics of Chinese civilization is the absence of castes; consequently, also, of a priestly, or purely theoretic, caste ; which could not exist, to begin with, except under a theological sanction. From this it results that the rich and enlightened class applies its activity to administration, to the actual government of society. In keeping with this social situation, minds of a purely theoretic cast are driven to direct their mental activity towards moral speculations directly connected with the government of society. Thus, under this two-fold influence, thinkers are wholly concerned with moral philosophy. It should be noted, too, that the nature of Morals or Ethic is perfectly suited for that. Ethic constitutes, for the theoretic class, the passage between theory and practice, being at once an art and a science. Its foundation touches on the highest theories, for it necessarily rests upon the knowledge of human nature; which itself finally rests upon the whole range of real scientific conceptions; by its culmination Ethic becomes directly practical, for it institutes the government of human nature. Ethic, or moral science, is theoretical as regards its foundation, practical as regards its immediate destination. It is clear that, under all aspects, strong intelligences found in such a study wherewithal to satisfy their true mental aptitudes while aiming at a real practical purpose, in conformity with the influence of their surroundings.

The outcome, then, of all this was a fundamental situation which prepared the way for and called forth the great work of Confucius; a work which has been an admirable success, in spite of the immense disturbances occasioned by the spread of Taoism and Buddhism. His constructive effort has been so grandly efficacious simply and solely because it was in keeping with the true evolutionary tenor of the civilization amidst which it was put forth; for Confucius's co-ordination is a moral and political co-ordination, and it was the kind of theory which such a situation imposed upon true thinkers.

But, furthermore, the special condition of China at the time when Confucius appeared gave a high immediate aim to his philosophic elaboration.

At the point of time when Confucius came upon the scene, a civilization, the leading features of which we have seen, was in existence simultaneously in several petty kingdoms, situated mainly in the basin of the Yellow River and a few adjacent districts like Shantung.

The common origin of the civilization prevalent in these several petty states is evidenced by their acknowledgment of a sort of subordination, more apparent than real, to the dynasty of Chow, which perpetuated, with some unavoidable changes, the family which inaugurated Chinese civilization. Again, military contests, of no little severity, were of

F

frequent occurrence amongst these divers petty kingdoms.   Here, then, we have to notice a two-fold fact—a real similitude of civilization co-existing with a state of political decomposition, or in other words, one and the same state of society co-existing in several neighboring countries, more or less independent and continually in conflict one with another. It is clear that such a situation must have impelled the nobler spirits to endeavour to put an end to such disorder, and to bring back union and order amongst peoples having like habits and ideas yet carried away by constantly recurring outbreaks.   This task might have been well or ill performed ; that depended on the sort of organ who might arise to fulfil the function ; but at all events here was a situation that called for some such effort ; and it was to this great function that Confucius devoted himself.   He sought, in fact, to act upon the rulers, the ministers of those several governments, in the name of a moral doctrine which should be simply a systematization, more or less abstract, of the whole of the antecedents of Chinese civilization.   That was the great problem he wanted to solve ; and he solved it.   Then he sought, by active preaching of his moral and political doctrine, to bring the rulers to put an end to the permanent anarchy of their military struggles and to the disorders of their inefficient internal administration.   He thus aimed at giving an ever increasing preponderance to a pacific and industrial civilization in keeping with the common antecedents of the several peoples.

Having now pointed out, Gentlemen, what was the nature of this great task, how the situation called for it, how the sum of the antecedents formed a preparation for it ; in a word, having definitely indicated the necessary scope of the work, we have next to see how it was accomplished by the organ whom the whole social destinies of his country charged with such a function.

K'ung Fu-tsze (Confucius) was born 551 years before Christ, in the little Kingdom of Lu, which was a part of the present province of Shan-tung.   He died in his native state 479 B.C., in the seventy-third year of his age.   His father was governor of Tsow, a town of the third rank, in the district of Ch'ang-p'ing, in the province of Shantung.   He lost his father early, and was brought up under the intelligent and devoted direction of his mother.   Educated with great care, he displayed from his boyhood's years that combination of intelligence, of veneration and devotedness which mark this noble character. At the age of seventeen, he accepted, at his mother's desire, a petty official appointment; as inspector of the grain and provision market. In this modest and useful post he displayed great firmness and that constant concern for the public interest which was the guiding principle of his life. He married when he was nineteen, at his mother's desire ; and soon after, at the age of twenty-one, he obtained a higher post in the public administration, Inspector General of the fields and flocks, with full powers to make any reforms in that department he might think advisable. At the age of twenty-four, just as his official career was beginning to blossom, he lost his mother. Thereupon, in conformity with the old customs, then too much neglected, but which it was his aim to strengthen and develop, he gave up all public employment, and devoted three years to a seclusion which he knew how to nobly utilize. It was then that he definitively conceived his great project of reform. In that fruitful three years of retreat into privacy he sketched the plan of his work, and betook himself to earnest study of Chinese antiquity, of divers moral and political questions, and to meditations that were indispensable to the accomplishment of his grand mission. His period of mourning over, he put the finishing touch to his long studies by journeys which he made into the divers kingdoms of China situated along the course of the Yellow River ; he gained, by attentive observation, a thorough understanding of the various countries which he wished to convert to his doctrine ; a doctrine which, indeed, was nothing but a philosophic systematization of the traditions and tendencies of Chinese civilization. We then see him for twenty years traversing these petty kingdoms, making disciples, being consulted by kings and their ministers, and continually persuading them to exercise a paternal, moral and pacific sway over the populations subject to them. It can be shown that the action of Confucius was, as Père Amiot has observed, not extended beyond the limits of a portion of the basin of the Yellow River, wherein Chinese civilization first arose and whence it gradually spread. "On the North side the tract in ques- "tion did not reach further than the frontier of Pechili ; it did not cross "the Kiang river on the South ; the province of Shantung was its limit "on the Eastern side, and the province of Shensi was its remotest "boundary on the West."—(G. Pauthier, China.)

Returning to his native state he consented, on the invitation of the Duke of Lu, to resume service in the administration ; and at the age of fifty he was promoted to the high office of Minister of Civil and Criminal Justice, thus exemplifying that combination of political life with theoretic studies of morals and history which was to become the characteristic of his school. Indeed this union of practice with theory is simply a necessary mode of systematizing the modifying element of Chinese civilization. In the exercise of his high functions he displayed from the outset that energetic firmness without which modificatory action would be impossible. He began, in fact, by demanding the death of the leading political functionary of the preceding administration, so as to concentrate upon the principal culprit an indispensable chastisement, and to prove at the same time his irrevocable resolution to prevent any new betrayal of trust. He brought to the discharge of his high duties that active goodness and devotion to the general welfare which in him were always conjoined with energy ; without which goodness is apt to miscarry. The Chinese historians have carefully recorded the details of his administration; and, besides his own work, we find his disciples at the same time attaining, in the various kingdoms, to important administrative and political posts, whilst others continued their master's philosophical and moral propaganda. On the death of his protector, the ruler of Lu, he withdrew from public affairs, and again bidding farewell to his native state, accompanied by some of his disciples, he continued his philosophical and social excursions into the various other petty kingdoms of China. At length, after fourteen years of absence, he returned to the country of his birth and devoted the last years of his life entirely to the definitive elaboration of his doctrine, and to the making of disciples who should continue it after him. The number of his followers largely increased, and they were scattered over the various principalities into which China proper was then split up. About the age of sixty-six he lost his wife ; soon after that his son also, and lastly his kinsman and favourite disciple Yen Hwei, to whom his chief regard was given, because he saw in him humanity, the greatest of all the virtues. Thus saddened were the closing years of the great reformer's life. Some time before his death he called together his principal disciples and gave them his last recommendations as regards the spirit of his doctrine and the conditions

of its application. "The sapless herb," said he, "is now entirely
"dried up, and I have no where to set me down to rest ; the sound
"doctrine had wholly disappeared, it had been utterly forgotten ; I have
"endeavoured to recall it and to re-establish its sway. I have not been
"successful. Will any one be found, after my death, willing to take
"upon himself this painful task ?"

His disciples performed his funeral rites with pious care ; and they
instituted the custom of an annual pilgrimage to the tomb of the great
reformer.

His school grew, his influence increased, and honours gradually
waxing were accorded to the memory of one of the most noble natures
of whom Humanity can boast ; of the man who has most strongly influenced Chinese civilization ;—influenced, that is to say, the destinies of
many hundreds of millions of men. The real worship of Confucius
began under the founder of the Han dynasty, which was a reparatory
and progressive dynasty. Soon temples were raised to Confucius in the
principal towns of China. It was under Chêu Tsung, the third emperor
of the Sung dynasty (998 A. D.) that the cult of Confucius was definitively constituted. "Under the Han dynasty he was named *Kung* or
"Duke ; the Tang dynasty named him the First Saint, and afterwards
"the Preacher Prince ; his statue likewise was clothed with a royal robe
"and a crown was placed upon its head. Under the Ming dynasty he
"was named the *most holy*, the *wisest* and the *most virtuous of the founders*
"*of men.*"

And lastly, his direct descendants, by a unique exception from the
general rule, obtained the title of hereditary nobles, which they still enjoy.

Such are the main features in the life of this great man. We must
now form an estimate of what his work amounted to as a whole.

There are, strictly speaking, scarcely any works of Confucius ;
besides the compilation of the ancient literary monuments of China, a
compilation which constitutes the sacred books properly so called, we
have, from his own hand, an historical fragment of the annals of his
native state, and, under the name of Confucian books, certain works
edited by his immediate disciples, which contain not merely his theories,
but sometimes even his very words.

The four principal works denominated Confucian are the *Hiao*

King or classic of Filial Piety, the *Ta Hio* or Great Lore, the *Chung Yung* or the Constant Mean, and the *Lun Yu* or Philosophic Discourses. The two first works, the *Hiao King* and the *Ta Hio*, were drawn up by Tsêng Tsze, an immediate disciple of Confucius. Tsêng Tsze, like his master, was born in the state of Lu (modern province of Shantung), in in the town of Wu south. He was forty-six years younger than Confucius. He was born, consequently, 505 B.C.

The *Chung Yung* or Constancy in the Mean, was drawn up by Tsze-sze, grandson of Confucius, through whom the family line of the sage was continued. Tsze-sze was thirty-seven years of age when his grandfather died. The *Lun Yu* or Philosophical Discourses were compiled by some of Confucius's disciples.

I proceed to give some quotations from these several works, (the *Ta Hio*, the *Chung Yung* and *Lun Yu*), in order that we may the better seize the general spirit of the philosophical and moral systematization of China's greatest sage.

The Ta Hio is made up of an argument, ascribed to Confucius, and an explanation due to Tsông Tsze, one of his disciples. This short work has been made the subject of numerous commentaries by the philosophers of China. The most notable, which is also most frequently printed along with the text, is that of Chu Hi, the celebrated schoolman of the Sung dynasty, who lived in the latter part of the twelfth century. In the Ta Hio the fundamental problem of moral perfectionment is neatly stated by Confucius :—

" The Great Lore treats of the way to make bright virtue brighter, " to win the people's love, and to stay in the utmost goodness. From " the Emperor down to the common folk there is one duty for all :— " to make the regulation of their conduct the first concern."

Here we have, in precise terms clearly stated, the supreme problem ; the moral perfectionment of each individual, that is the end to be aimed at. The task of moral philosophy is to shape and organize this process of perfectionment. Confucius conceives, in a general way, the mental conditions of the solution of the problem as follows :—

" Things have their main points and minor points ; affairs have " their issues and origins. To have a knowledge of what comes first " and what afterwards is a near approach to the way in question."

" The first thing is to know your aim, and then form a resolve ;
" your resolve being formed, then be steadfast in it ; being steadfast,
" you will have peace of mind ; having peace of mind, you can then
" meditate ; meditating, you can attain your aim."

Confucius, therefore, without concerning himself in any way
whatever about the supernatural, thus formulates, in distinct and precise
terms, a statement of the definitive problem of man's destiny : to attain,
by moral perfectionment, the state of full unity, employing intelligence
to discover the conditions and the means of attainment. The commentary of his disciple Tseng Tsze is intended to work out these
fundamental ideas, and to connect them with the early history and most
venerable traditions of, China in such a way as to maintain and
consolidate the social continuity ; instead of breaking it, as other
reformers hitherto have done, in a revolutionary spirit and methods.

" How profound," says the commentary, " was King Wan's endea-
" vour, unwearied and ardent, to attain the highest goodness ! As a
" sovereign, his aim was to be beneficent ; as a subject, his aim was to
" be reverential ; as a son, his aim was to be filial ; as a father, his aim
" was loving kindness ; in his intercourse with statesmen his guiding
" aim was good faith." Here we see illustrated in what this moral
perfectionment, the supreme aim of existence, consists : to bring the
various natural relations under the controlling sway of humanity,
submissiveness, filial piety, tenderness and sincerity.

The precise conception of the state of perfection, as Confucius
understood it, is clearly and definitely set forth in the Chung Yung or
Constancy in the Mean, the work, as I have already stated, of his
grandson Tsze-sze.

In this work, the most systematic of all the Confucian books, Tsze-
sze works out the mental conditions and propounds the moral co-ordination from which results the type of perfection which ought, under all
vicissitudes, to be striven after, but the realization of which is only
attained in exceptional cases by men destined for the moral or political
government of societies.

Let us see, first of all, what is Confucius's conception of the type
of the Sage, or the man who has realized the ideal of perfection. I
quote literally from the Chung Yung.

"It is only the Sage of widest ken who can fully understand and
"develop his own nature; being able to fully understand and develop his
"own nature, he can therefore fully understand and develop the nature of
"other men; being able fully to understand and develop the nature of
"other men, he can therefore fully understand and develop the nature of
"things (animate and inanimate); being able fully to understand and
"develop the nature of things (animate and inanimate), he can therefore
"co-operate with Heaven and Earth in their transforming and sustaining
"operations; being able to co-operate with Heaven and Earth in their
"transforming and sustaining operations, he can therefore constitute
"himself with Heaven and Earth, a trinity."

"Next to the perfect Sage comes he who by culture rectifies his
"nature flawed by some ingrained bias."

The perfect man, then, is one who, swayed by moral propensities,
arrives, by knowledge of the natural laws of living and of inorganic
bodies, at the power of regularly modifying the natural order in such a
way as, by his systematic intervention, to make it more perfect. It was
thus that Confucius framed the noble ideal of that modifying power
which, according to his own fine expression, constitutes a third over-
ruling agency intermediate between Heaven and Earth. Herein we have,
as it were, a deep presentiment of the normal order; of which, in fact,
a leading feature will be an active perfecting of the natural order, under
the impulsion of an all-absorbing social feeling. Confucius recognizes
the general laws of the activity of Heaven and Earth as the foundation
upon which rests all wise endeavour to modify the spontaneously existing
order of things.

We observe that Confucius, in perfecting the fetishistic and sky-
worshiping civilization from which he sprung, borrows, for his political
and moral systematization, from the laws of Heaven and Earth that type
of order and of regularity which he seeks to achieve in human life by the
habitual preponderance of the social over the selfish feelings; such
preponderance being the sole means of realizing in the human order that
type of regularity furnished by observation of the external world. A
quotation from a characteristic passage will convincingly show that it
was indeed under the impulsion of fetishistic observation of the natural
laws of the world that Confucius constructed his type of order.

"Confucius," says Tsze-sze, "possessed, as if by hereditary trans-
"mission, the virtues of Yaou and Shun, and modelled himself on Wăn
"and Wu as his exemplars. Above, he kept in unison with the seasons
"of the sky; below, he conformed to the water and the land.

"We may liken him unto the sky and earth in respect of the
"universality with which they uphold and sustain things, the univer-
"sality with which they overspread and enfold things. We may liken
"him unto the four seasons in respect of their varied march, unto
"the sun and moon in respect of their alternate shining.

"All things are kept in train together without their injuring one
"another; their ways go on together without interfering one with an-
"other; the smaller forces, in river streams, the greater forces, in ample
"transformations. It is this that makes the sky and earth so great."

Thus it is the external order which furnishes at once the type of all
regularity, and the starting point and necessary condition of all sus-
ceptibility of modification. But this modificatory action can and should
only be exerted under the guidance of a systematic moral plan. Let us
look somewhat more closely into the general features of that moral
systematization of which I mentioned merely the fundamental principle;
the preponderance of sociality over selfishness.

"There are five universal ways, or lines of duty; and three means
whereby to pursue them; to wit: as between lord and vassal, as between father and son, as between husband and wife, as between elder
and younger brother, as associating with friends—these five are the
"universal ways (or duties). Knowledge, humanity, courage; these
"are the three universal virtues; and it is by their unity that the duties
are carried into practice."

Chu Hi, (who flourished towards the close of the twelfth century
of the Christian era), in his commentary on the *Chung Yung*, regards
the cardinal thesis of that work to be that *wisdom, humanity* (or
universal benevolence) and *force of character* are the three virtues of
capital and universal importance; the door, so to speak, through which
lies the entrance to that right path which all men ought to follow. We
may take it, then, as a Confucian tenet that the faculties necessary for
the attainment of that state of moral perfection which admits of
entire devotion of self to the service of all are—wisdom, humanity and

courage. In keeping with this conception is the ideal portrait which Confucius draws of the statesman continuously devoted to the service of society.

"All who have to govern the empire with its constituent and depen-
"dent states have nine canons of conduct :—to cultivate self-control ; to
"exalt the worthy ; to keep on intimate terms with their relatives ; to
"accord to the great vassals due respect; to be in sympathy with the
"whole body of vassals ; to treat the villeins as children ; to attract all
"kinds of artificers ; to be indulgent to commorant strangers ; and to
"cherish the barons of the fiefs.

"Let but self-control be cultivated and the path of the social duties
"is established, etc."

Besides framing this moral system, Confucius still farther promoted the great object of his life by editing the ancient literary monuments of Chinese civilization. The result of his labours in this field are
the sacred books of China ; these are the Yih King, or Book of Changes ;
the Shû King, or Book of Historical Documents ; the Shih King, or Book
of Poetry ; and the Lî Kî, or Record of Rites. To these a fifth was
added, from Confucius's own pen, the Chun Chu, or Spring and Autumn,
containing the annals of his native state of Lu.

The Shih King, or Book of Poetry, is a collection of over three
hundred ancient poems or songs, a few of which date so far back as the
Shang dynasty (B. C. 1766—1123), but the others range from the foundation of the Chow dynasty in the twelfth century B. C. till within a
generation or two of Confucius's own day.

The Lî Kî, or Record of Rites, contains a vast collection of rules relating to the constitution of the governing body and the duties pertaining
to each office, as well as maxims and regulations as to the behaviour
of the officials on the occasions of the various social and civil ceremonies. Although containing many documents of high antiquity, this
work received its present shape, some centuries after Confucius, at the
hands of scholars of the Han dynasty.

The Yih King, or Book of Changes, is one of the most ancient monuments of Chinese civilization. The framework of it is as follows. First
come the eight trigrams of Fuh-Hi, to whom tradition ascribes the
foundation of the nation ; and these sets of whole and bisected lines are,

by duplication and combination with one another, expanded into sixty-four hexagrams. Then comes a short explanatory text to each hexagram, appended, as it is said, by Wen Wang, founder of the Chow dynasty, who probably followed some ancient tradition, the purport of which has not otherwise been transmitted to us. Chow Kung, son of Wen Wang, added some further observations : and upon this triple textual foundation Confucius made a commentary still more extensive. Thus built up, the Yih King has been the subject of an uninterrupted series of commentaries down to our own day. Many a mind in China, attracted by the spell of primitive obscurity of meaning, has been exercised over the interpreting of this book. One thing that is plainly to be seen in the Yih King is the employment of number as a means of explaining and regulating the affairs of life ; a tendency we meet with in all early civilizations. Numeration, established during the prevalence of Fetishism, constitutes the first scientific institution of Humanity ; and there is a sort of natural tendency to reduce to these first positive notions all our notions of other kinds. Hence arises that philosophic theory of the influence of numbers which we so often meet with ; and which, in spite of the exaggerations incident to the applications made of it, contains a greater amount of truth and a higher social and mental importance than is nowadays commonly supposed.

The most important of the four sacred books collated by Confucius is the Shu King, or Book of History, containing information of the greatest historical interest respecting the ancient dynasties of China. The period covered by this work extends from the Emperors Yao and Shun (2357 B. C.) to the year 790 B. C. The authentic history of China, say the critics, does not go further back than the twenty-fourth century before Christ. Beyond that date we, are landed in the mythical or semi-mythical ages. So Confucius, in addition to his direct task of systematizing the morals of his nation, edited, if he did not collect, its fundamental historical traditions. And rightly did he regard himself as the perpetuator of those traditions ; for in effect his moral teaching transmitted them in a more perfect form, instead of condemning and rejecting them.

We can now sum up shortly the work accomplished by Confucius, and our estimate of his character and place in history.

We see, to begin with, a great philosopher, intent upon producing a vast moral and social development, taking his stand, fast and firm, upon the whole aggregate of antecedents and traditions. It is not here a question of arbitrary hypotheses like those by means of which Christianity constructed for itself an artificial tradition, in default of the ability to faithfully represent, by a sound scientific theory, the antecedents out of which it actually arose. Here it is a philosopher taking his stand, frankly and fully, upon the whole series of the antecedents of Chinese civilization and aiming to promote thereby its systematic development. This is an example of the proper, the normal philosophic type, in closest conformity to the true scientific spirit, which always rests its present constructions upon the constructions that have preceded. Under the Christian and revolutionary impulsion, Westerns, in their moral and social speculations have, on the contrary, manifested a decided tendency, as unreasonable as it is immoral, to take no account whatever of social continuity.

Confucius finds his starting point in sky-worshiping Fetishism, the basis of Chinese civilization. Fully accepting this astrolatric Fetishism, and deeply respecting the cult founded thereupon, he commences to operate in this Fetishism a transformation which will be fully realised amongst the most distinguished of his successors. He begins to work out, in fact, the distinction between activity and life. Fetishism considers all beings not only as active, (therein it is scientifically correct), but also as alive, which is true only in respect of a certain limited number of them.

Confucius is evidently far more concerned about the *ways* or laws of the Sky and Earth than about the *wills* of those two overruling beings. Hence, although the commandment is conceived as a *mandate* of the Sky, this *mandate* comes to mean not so much the celestial will as the fatality which result from regular laws. And this conception of Confucius's is all the more important in that he gives to it the widest generality by regarding all the phenomena of society as regulated by the laws of celestial phenomena. To a certain degree, undoubtedly, they are so. Astronomical conditions have an influence upon social conditions, but not of that exact kind that must at first have been supposed. We thus find, afterwards, eminent minds of the Confucian School tending spontaneously towards the scientific stage of thought, owing to their belief that all bodies are active, but not all alive; a point of view more reasonable than that of theologians and metaphysicians who regard matter as inert.

On the basis furnished by the worship of the Sky Confucius constructed his moral system, borrowing from the fetishistic worship of the Sky those notions of *order* and *submission* which celestial phenomena are so well fitted to suggest. Thereon he rested his coördination of morals, fully conscious of the grand political and social destination of his work. His aim was a practical, working system of morals, in which the duties proper to the various relations of human life should be clearly defined ; always keeping in view the chief end of man, that state of full spiritual unity in which social feelings have preponderance over the selfish. And the means by which he solved the problem was by giving the position of pre-eminent importance to the institution of the Family, based as it is upon submission on the part of the children and devotedness on the part of the parents.

Such, stated in the most general terms, is the plan of his moral system. It is, as you see, completely untrammelled by any concern for the supernatural. I have already explained, in my first lecture, how that is due to the absence of the theological spirit, and to the persistence with which the régime of fetishistic sky-worship held its ground.

Referring to this complete absence of supernatural beliefs, a very distinguished man, M. Abel Remusat, has stated that the moral system of Confucius is wanting as regards a sanction. It is an astonishing circumstance that so able a thinker should have so far allowed himself to be led away by theologico-metaphysical prejudices as not to see that this pretended lack of sanction is just what gives the stamp of reality and nobleness to Confucius's moral system. For the absence of a *supernatural sanction*, which is always of the selfish kind, only brings out all the more prominently the formal admission, by Confucius, of the spontaneous existence of benevolent sentiments in human nature. Confucius acknowledges that human nature is spontaneously moral. The sanction is just the happiness of doing what is good because it is good; it is the attainment of that state of full unity which the truly wise man pursues

as his ideal, under the impulse of ardent regard for others, enlightened
by high thought.   On this point theologico-metaphysical conceptions
have helped to debase the true notion of human nature ; especially since
the practical wisdom of the clergy has ceased to remedy the defects
inherent in their doctrine.

Lastly, in a political point of view, the gradual development of the
Confucian reformation has had, for its results, the giving of a solid
constitution to the class by which Chinese civilization is modified, the
assuring and perfecting of the action of that class, and the enduring and
ever increasing efficacy of its influence.

Such, in short outline, is the sum of what was effected by that noble
life, systematically and actively devoted to the working out of a great
social reform.

No doubt Western civilization has superior types to show us,
whether as regards intelligence or activity, to that of the philosopher of
China.   Aristotle and Archimedes were intellects of a higher order ;
Cæsar was a statesman of incomparably greater force.   But we may
affirm that the West furnishes no type that realized, to the same degree
as Confucius, the combination of sound judgment and morality with
activity long and unweariedly devoted to the general amelioration of
society.   Here was a philosopher who, without taking advantage of
any superstitious dogma to prop up his system, proclaiming moral
perfectionment as the supreme aim, and making it consist in continuous
devotedness to society, of which he tried to improve the foundations,
nevertheless in no way broke with the traditions of the civilization upon
which he sought to act, and gave as the sanction for such a life of effort,
the deep sense of duty done.

Assuredly it will be an instructive lesson to Occidentals to
contemplate such a type.   They can learn from it something very
different from what, in their unreasonable ingratitude, Christians and
revolutionary thinkers are wont to believe.   They can learn, that is to
say, the feasibility of pursuing social progress without breaking with
predecessors, and that all the more worthily do we modify a society
when we skilfully lean for support upon those who have been in the
field before us and do full justice to their work.

Then the West, enlightened and regenerated, will be more and more inclined to assign a place amongst the objects of its profound veneration to the illustrious philosopher whom an immense and ancient empire proclaims as the foremost of its reformers.

Let us now examine Confucius's system, on its own merits, and in its relation to the definitive co-ordination of human knowledge.

Confucius's theory is, in its essence, an empirical co-ordination of morals, having for its immediate aim the directing of human nature aright. Now the immense defect of such a co-ordination is just the defect of Chinese civilization itself; that is to say, the absence of such a sufficient development of abstract science as should form the systematic foundation for morals, and furnish an adequate power of modificatory action over the external world and over man himself. For the ability to modify rests entirely upon the knowledge of abstract laws. It is only when the abstract laws of the various phenomena have been clearly ascertained that it becomes possible to institute a course of modificatory action over them of a powerful and regular kind.

By way of showing more distinctly what a tremendous gap the co-ordination of Confucius presents, I shall contrast it with that encyclopedic series into which Auguste Comte has condensed the whole body of abstract science. In that hierarchical arrangement the abstract sciences are placed in the following order :

Mathematics, Astronomy, Physics, Chemistry, Biology, Sociology, Morals. Moral Science, the crowning achievement of this mental evolution, is composed of two distinct parts; first, Theoretic Morals, which is concerned with the knowledge of human nature; secondly, Practical Morals, which is concerned with the government of human nature. It is by means of this second part that the passage from theory to practice is effected ; and indeed it would be correct to say that, in the long run, there are no mere theoricians, but only practicians, of whom some work upon things and the others upon men. But the necessarily systematic character of action of the latter sort has had the effect of giving to those who are concerned with it the designation of *theoretic class.*

This contrast will be sufficient to show the profound lacuna which, owing to the very nature of Chinese civilization, exists in the systematization of Confucius. It wants that long abstract elaboration, beginning with mathematics and ascending to morals, without which it is impossible to establish a true and sufficiently profound theory of human nature. But this theoretic defect is, as regards the government of human nature, a source of serious insufficiency; for man, social being that he is, cannot be sufficiently directed without a well-grounded knowledge of the abstract laws of the various phenomena which exercise sway over him, from mathematical phenomena up to social. Now the ulterior evolution of China has not succeeded in filling up this gap; the very nature of Chinese civilization being antipathetic to the spontaneous institution of abstraction; and therefore quite unfit for the scientific elaborations required. The philosophic work done by the school of Confucius amounts to nothing more than the development of certain points and the production of commentaries.

The analysis we have thus made shows the profound mental and social insufficiency of the great empirical systematization of Confucius; but it shows at the same time in what way the West will be able to act, through its most eminent organs, upon such a civilization. Western science, accepting, as Confucius did, the supremacy of morals, will soon succeed in making clear to the directing minds of that civilization, the necessity of supplying, for its consolidation and support, a foundation which will allow of its at last instituting an adequate government of human nature. And besides this common platform of the supremacy of morals, the constantly increasing contacts of the West and China will bring the philosophic minds of that great empire to perceive the need of a science of society, capable of justly estimating social states so different as those of China and the West; the felt want of sociology will then gradually lead on to the recognition of the need of biological knowledge, and so on along the successive links of that indivisible chain formed by the interconnections of the several distinct orders of phenomena, chemical, physical, astronomical, mathematical. The result of all this, in short, will be, that Chinese philosophers will have to study, systematically, the grand hierarchy of the abstract sciences, the essential basis of the definitive mental state of the human species. Positivism, holding in respect the spontaneous evolution of China, will thus bring about a complete renovation of its mental state; and it will do this all the better in that, incorporating Fetishism into its own system, it will adopt, in its essence, the Chinese official cult.

We must now briefly advert to the principal works that have emanated from the school of Confucius, or rather to the general spirit by which those works are characterized. Our concern is not with a detailed history of Chinese philosophy and science ; that would be an immense subject, of but small interest to us here ; the important thing for us is to see what is their essential character. A thorough study of Chinese historians might furnish us with new details ; but extensive works have already been published on this subject, amply sufficient to allow of our constructing, in accordance with the general laws of the philosophy of history, a sound scientific theory of this mental evolution. Three kinds of works emanate from the school of Confucius, deeply stamped with the traits of Chinese civilization, such as we have depicted it. First, moral works, developing the doctrines of Confucius ; secondly, works of a natural philosophy, which transforms the astrolatric Fetishism by separating the idea of activity from that of life, and in so doing builds upon the foundation which Confucius himself laid ; lastly, immense works of erudition, statistics, etc., etc., in a word, works of concrete sociology. For these works of erudition are, in substance, collections of observations which form material on which genuine scientific works on sociology may be based. For Chinese civilization, true to its peculiar concrete spirit, has not advanced beyond works of this preparatory kind.

Let us glance, first, at the works of moral philosophy.

These works are nothing more, in fact, than commentaries, numerous and ponderous, on Confucius. They explain and develop the formulæ of the empiric systematization of that great reformer ; but they in no way change its fundamental spirit and features. The system of public examinations is based on the study of the Confucian books of morals, and this fact has naturally given a stimulus to the production of this immense literature of commentators. The principal philosopher who advanced along the path opened up by Confucius was Meng-tsze (Mencius). Mencius was born about the beginning of the fourth century B. C. in what is now the province of Shantung ; he died at a great age, 314 B. C. In the estimation of the Chinese he ranks, justly, immediately after Confucius. Public honours are rendered to him similar to those given to Confucius himself ; with whom, indeed, he is

G

always associated in the people's veneration. There is one peculiar
trait in Mencius which constitutes a distinct improvement upon the
system of Confucius, though it existed there in germ. He has formulated,
more explicitly than Confucius did, the conditions under which the
elimination of the imperial family, the central element of union, becomes
a matter of necessity. He lays it down that, when the ruling house no
longer fulfils its fundamental function in a tolerable way, it must then
be got rid of; when the head of that family ceases to discharge the
moral and social duties attaching to his position, he thereupon ceases
to be the sovereign, the son of the Sky. The mandate of the Sky, in
virtue whereof he governs, must be withdrawn from him. There is
thus, in Mencius, a spirit of direct antagonism to any encroachments or
irregularities on the part of the imperial power. All important though
it be, as the element of the unity, maintenance and spread of Chinese
civilization, it must, nevertheless, sometimes be necessary to change the
central organ of the society; and it is this necessity which Mencius has
fully and directly dealt with. It is easy to see how far removed is
such a spirit from that absolute submission which pure theologism
engenders.

Amongst the numerous commentators on Confucius, special mention
should be made of Chu Hi, who lived in the latter part of the twelfth
century of the Christian era, under the dynasty of the Sung. Chu Hi
became *the* classical commentator; and his work is generally printed
along with the text of the Confucian books. This commentary is full of
wisdom and good sense; as, indeed, most of the Chinese commentators
are when their minds are not weakened by the theological fancies of the
Buddhist and Taoist systems. These works of moral philosophy,
consisting of commentaries on the fundamental Chinese books, continue
to be produced even to the present day, and several of the Emperors
even have deigned to add their contributions to the series.

Confucius had marked the distinction between activity and life.
That distinction forms the starting point whence arose a Natural
Philosophy intermediate between Fetishism and Science. Chu Hi thus
founded an atomistic philosophy, in which he demonstrates, for
cultivated minds, the separation, in bodies, of the idea of activity from
that of life, which Confucius had sketched. Phenomena are no longer,

as in pure Fetishism, the result of the wills of the beings in which they are manifested; they are merely a result of the variety of the modes of activity of those beings. He thus admits that the special activity of each of these beings produces the various phenomena; the manifestation of this special activity being rendered regular by the preponderant activity of the Sky. This amounts to a positive transformation of the primitive astrolatric Fetishism of China; and the conception has this advantage, that it properly assigns to astronomical phenomena a normal preponderance over all others. He goes on to extend, though in an exaggerated way, this preponderance to the field of social phenomena, the evolutions of which he connects with the celestial movements. It does not admit of dispute that animal, vegetable and social existence are powerfully controlled by these, the most general of the laws of the world.

Thus, in such a philosophy, the notion of supernatural beings exterior to the real beings and producing in them, at their caprice, the several phenomena, is wholly absent; everything is explained by the spontaneous activity of the beings themselves. Such a conception comes very close to that on which true science rests; all that is wanting in it is the institution of scientific abstraction. After all, in what does real scientific systematization consist, but in accepting the spontaneous activity of the various beings and in investigating the abstract laws of their several modes of activity, in so far as they are shared by a great number of different individuals?

The Chinese have also a considerable number of works of Natural History; that is to say, of collections of observations relating to the various beings; but these notices, very numerous and very detailed, are essentially concrete, savouring too much of practical purposes; and they have not led up to any genuine biological law. Meteorological observations, too, precise and abundant, have been collected and set down. Their astronomy is of the same stamp; observations many in number and not wanting in precision, but purely concrete. Such theories as it contains—and they are very imperfectly developed—come from the Mussulman and Christian astronomers.

In brief, there is, in their cosmological and biological studies, immense development of works of concrete observation, numerous and valuable; but of real abstract science there is none.

And this same feature, the inevitable consequence of the nature of Chinese civilization itself, characterizes their studies relative to social phenomena. We owe to the Chinese, in fact, admirable works of erudition ; that is to say, of concrete sociology.

Confucius had given attention to historical studies; for, besides editing the principal ancient books, he had himself compiled a history of the Kingdom of Lu. The sentiment of continuity, too, so strong in China, was an additional incentive to the cultivation of historic studies ; whilst the virtually positive spirit, free from supernatural beliefs, accounts for that exactitude and patient and critical correctness which characterizes the principal works of erudition of the Chinese savants ; fables and erratic flights, when they occur, are traceable to the disturbing influence of the Buddhists or Taoists.

Writers of the Confucian school have followed along this path of patient, exact historical studies ; and their works treat not only of China proper, but also of all the surrounding peoples with whom the Chinese have had commercial or political relations. It is in this rich mine of Chinese historians that we must quarry in order to get positive and trustworthy knowledge of the history and geography of the Tartar peoples. I cannot and ought not to attempt here to give even a summary of the story of the immense works of erudition we owe to China ; all I can do is to dwell upon two types, by way of sample, and in order to give greater definiteness to the foregoing general remarks.

One of the most eminent of Chinese men of learning was Sze-ma Ts'ien, who has been styled the *Father of History*, and also the *Herodotus of China*. He was born at Lung-mên, in the province of Honan, about the year 168 B. C., under the dynasty of the Western Han—that is to say under that great restoring and re-establishing dynasty, which, whilst availing itself of the results of the energetic action of Ts'in She Hwangti, yet again took up, and carried forward the development of Chinese civilization in the spirit of its antecedents.

His father, who was the chief of the court historians, intended his son to be a writer of history, and educated him carefully with that view ; and the latter from his earliest years showed himself worthy of such a calling.

" He was put in command of a military expedition, which took

"him to the regions now known as Yunnan and Szechuen. On the
"march, he learned that his father, Sze-ma T'an, was dangerously ill.
"He lost not a moment in repairing to his side, but arrived only in time
"to receive his dying wishes.

"Even on his death-bed, Sze-ma T'an's sense of duty did not forsake
"him ; and his son's journey was a subject of interest to him, both as a
"father, and as a historian. He asked for a detailed account of it, and
"when he had heard it, he addressed his son in words which the latter
"has recorded at full length. 'The great historiographer,' said he, 'took
"'my hands in his, and with tears in his eyes, spoke as follows: Our
"'ancestors, since the time of the third dynasty, have always distinguished
"'themselves in the Academy of History. Is it to be my fate to see this
"'honorable succession come to an end? Should you succeed me, my son,
"'read the writings of our ancestors. The Emperor, who now gloriously
"'reigns over all China, has commanded me to take part in the solemn
"'ceremonies which he is about to celebrate on the sacred Mount. I am
"'unable to obey. Doubtless you will be ordered to discharge the duties.
"'Then remember my wishes. Filial piety is shown first in the perfor-
"'mance of duties towards parents, then in the rendering of service to
"'one's prince, and lastly, in care for one's own good fame. The crown
"'of filial piety is to bring home to a father and a mother, the glory
"'of a name become renowned.'"—(*Abel Remusat, New Asiatic Miscellanies, Vol. II.*)

Sze-ma Ts'ien fulfilled his father's behest. He became a historian,
was appointed Historiographer, and lastly a Censor. He had the double
duty of recording the past, and of counselling the present. He
discharged his censorial duties under very trying circumstances, and
with a heroism which did him honour. His historical work is of immense
extent, accurate, impartial, and marked by sober critical judgment.
It is a splendid monument of learning. The Sze Ki, or Historical
Record, as the work is entitled, is divided into 130 books, arranged in
five sections. The first, consisting of 12 books, contains, under the
heading "Imperial Records," all that relates to the Empire, considered
as a whole. The second, consisting of ten books, is made up of
historical lists, and synoptical tables, such as we have in plenty in the
West. The third, in eight books, is called Pa-shu (the eight branches

of knowledge), namely, Rites, Music, Harmony, Chronology, Astrology, Sacrificial Service, Water-courses, and Weights and Measures. Sze-ma Ts'ien here treats, in as many separate dissertations, of all the changes the above enumerated subjects have undergone, in the twenty-two centuries of history which his work embraces. The fourth section, forming thirty books, comprises the genealogical history of all the great land-holding families, from the great vassals of the Chow dynasty, to the plain ministers and generals of the Han. The fifth, and final section, made up of seventy books, includes geographical memoirs on foreign countries, and biographical notices, more or less detailed, of all persons of eminence in literature or administration.—(*Abel Remusat, New Asiatic Miscellanies.*)

The literati in China have written a great number of encyclopedias, some general, others special. Some of them relate to the various occupations, such as agriculture, sericulture, and ceramics, etc., etc. Others relate to different branches of administration, the superintendence of the public granaries, the planning and management of watercourses, etc. One of the most eminent Chinese encyclopedists was Ma Twan-lin. Ma Twan-lin was born in the province of Kwangsi, about the middle of the thirteenth century. His master was the celebrated commentator Chu Hi, of whom we have already spoken.

The fall of the Sung dynasty and the Mongul conquest led him to decide to devote himself entirely to writing learned works, and give up all thoughts of an official career. He gave twenty years to the composition of the great work, which, under the title of Antiquarian Researches, constitutes his claim to fame.

This vast encyclopedia consists of twenty-four sections, divided into 848 books. I proceed to give a list of them, taken from Abel Remusat.

1. Of the division of lands, and their produce under different dynasties, 7 books.
2. Of money, metallic, token, or paper, 2 books.
3. Of the population, and its fluctuations, 2 books.
4. Of Administration, 2 books.
5. Of tolls, customs, dues, and taxes in general, and octroi, etc., 6 books.

6. Trade and barter, 2 books.
7. Of Land tax, 1 book.
8. Of State expenditure, 5 books.
9. Of Promotion and rank of magistrates, 12 books.
10. Of Studies and the State examinations, 7 books.
11. Of Duties of Magistrates, 21 books.
12. Of Sacrifices, 25 books.
13. Of Ancestral Temples, 15 books.
14. Of Court Ceremonial, 22 books.
15. Of Music, 15 books.
16. Of War, 16 books.
17. Of Punishment and Torture, 12 books.
18. Of Books Classical and other, 76 books.

This section is so extensive by reason of its comprising analyses of a host of curious treatises on all sorts of subjects; it is, in fact, a compendium of the whole range of Chinese literature.

19. Chronology and genealogies of the successive dynasties, 18 books.
20. Of the tributary principalities and fiefs, under the several dynasties, 18 books.
21. Of Heavenly bodies, and what happens amongst them, as eclipses, conjunctions, etc., 17 books.
22. On Portents, Calamities, as Floods, Earthquakes, Ærolites, showers of insects (vermin), 20 books.
23. Of the Geography of China, and its political divisions at different epochs of the monarchy, 9 books.
24. Of the Geography of Foreign countries and of all the peoples known to the Chinese, 25 books.

Supplements to this vast work have been written on the same plan, continuing up to the present day.

The author of this huge undertaking was born about 1245 after Christ, and died about 1325.

These two specimens will serve to fix more definitely in our minds a clear idea of what Chinese science is, such as it has been developed, mainly by the Confucian school.

Concrete, special, exact, accurate studies, but absence of science properly so called; for that always consists in the discovery of the abstract laws of phenomena. And this essential character, the outcome of the very nature of Chinese civilization itself, has never been perceptibly modified, either by the abstract metaphysical aberrations of the Taoists, or even by the introduction of the various elements of abstract science, by the Hindus, Mussulmans or Christians. It is only the demonstrated religion, based on the dogmatic co-ordination of the several abstract sciences from Mathematics up to Morals that can bring about a thorough yet regular change.

THE RELATIONS OF THE WEST WITH CHINA.

We have thus brought to a close our estimate of Chinese civilization, having regard first to its essential elements, then to its historical development, and lastly to its principal philosophic types. The task was a highly important one from a theoretic point of view. For China has been hitherto a sort of historical mystery—wholly inexplicable by all the theological and metaphysical theories that have been attempted.[1] There were no doubt plenty of documents, due to a deep and patient erudition : some interesting and even at times profound views had been put forth ; but there was no such thing as a genuine theory of Chinese civilization considered as a whole. A striking proof of this is the fact that one who had given so much thought to the subject as Abel Remusat made such a mistake as to suppose that metaphysicians, imbued with what was most likely a Hindoo philosophy, were the types of Chinese civilization ; in fact, Abel Remusat, in spite of his ingenious and even profound views, so far mistook the fundamental spirit of the people whom he had so carefully studied, that he could never understand that they actually worshiped the sky, although that worship underlies the whole of their long mental evolution.

Thus then this great historical problem had not been solved, and could not be, until the advent of the Positive Philosophy ; which was to demonstrate by such a solution its profound reality and fruitfulness.

But however great the philosophic importance of this theory, it will serve a still more useful purpose if we can derive from the consequences

---

[1] It is the profound Positive conception of Fetishism as the spontaneous starting-point of human reason that has furnished the clue to a really scientific theory of the subject.

that necessarily follow from it the foundations of a systematic policy which shall direct the ever multiplying relations of the West with China in such a way that those relations may be useful to both these great social groups, instead of being, as they manifestly are now, a source of demoralization to both alike.

It is, then, the principles of such a policy that I shall now proceed to deduce from the two-fold study of the evolutions of the West and of China: this will be the practical and social outcome of our long study.

Before entering on the explanation of this policy, I must briefly consider what is the present condition of the West, both in itself and as regards its relations with the rest of the world, and especially with China.   •

One first incontestable fact is the revolutionary state of the West; that is to say, there is the absence of a guiding doctrine, disregard of antecedents, straining after the future without respect to the past, an ever increasing intellectual anarchy. Unity of opinion, the basis of all lasting society, is rapidly disappearing. The West is thus placing itself more and more every day in an utterly unstable position.

The second capital fact of the situation is the increase of industrial activity, and of a spirit of daring enterprise, which aggravates, instead of counteracting, the absence of doctrinal unity above noted. We must ascertain the historical causes of these two main facts, before following up their consequences, as affecting the relations of the West with the rest of the world.

The middle ages, at the close of the 14th century, handed down to the dawning modern era a social mass that was free, without caste and necessarily pacific and industrial. The result was a state of affairs most favourable to the development of scientific, artistic and industrial activity. The situation which Auguste Comte has proved to have been the source of the free evolution of Greek civilization, became, thanks to the emancipation of the serfs effected by the middle ages, common to the numerous populations of Western Europe. The necessarily peaceful activity of the social body, the widespread ease and independence which it created, the freedom that accompanies the decay of the spirit of caste and of theocracy, became thenceforth the source of a hitherto unheard of activity, of an unexampled hardihood of enterprise,

which the acquired results only intensified, and which met with less and
less opposition from the gradually waning power of the theological
belief which had prevailed in the Middle ages. This movement, confined
exclusively to the peoples of the West, was the necessary outcome of
the series of their antecedents, Greek, Roman and Catholic-Feudal.

In was thus that the situation I have just described to you was
brought about :—An immense population given up to an activity ever on
the increase and ever less and less under control.[1]

Minds placed in such an environment were sure, perforce, to push
their enterprises in every direction. There were sure to arise, and there
did arise energetic individualities, putting forth the most powerful activity
in industry and in commerce. The glow thus kindled was certain, owing
to the combined impulsion of the scientific and industrial spirit, of
military habits, and in a minor degree of theological beliefs, to develop
active relations with the rest of the globe. The establishment of these
relations on the largest scale was as inevitable as it was indispensable.

The very situation which I have just analyzed, so favourable to
individual initiative, and to scientific and industrial development, explains
why it was that relations ever larger and more active were of necessity
developed between the West and the rest of the world, at the close of the
middle ages, and particularly from the 15th century. We see at that
epoch an unparalleled activity in voyaging hither and thither over the
earth. The planet was really discovered, and fully explored ; navigation
was improved ; and the geographical knowledge then acquired became
the incentive to new adventures.

---

[1] This group, composed of the five great populations, viz., France in the centre,
Italy and Spain in the south, Great Britain and Germany in the north, is habitually
designated by the name of Christendom. It would be opportune to substitute the
names Westerndom and Western peoples for the unsuitable denominations of Christendom and Christian peoples. In the first place, these antiquated designations are
not sufficiently precise, as covering also Russia and the Eastern Christians, who
do not properly belong to such a group. In the second place, those designations
indicate as unique in the establishment of Western civilization the influence of
Christianity ; whereas that assuredly was not even the leading influence. Lastly,
they tend to maintain a hateful dualism between the five advanced populations
and the rest of the globe. The substitution therefore of Westerndom for Christendom is both philosophically urgent and socially beneficial.

Here we have an all-important fact; we must accept it as the inevitable result of all that had gone before it. Whether this were a good thing or a bad, the fact could not have been otherwise, as I have just explained. But if these relations were inevitable, they were also indispensable, as well for the preparation as for the establishment of the Universal Religion, which the regenerated West was to build up.

The final aim of the more advanced portions of Humanity is the foundation of a Universal Religion. A grand attempt in this direction was made in the West, namely Catholicism; and though it has been a complete failure as regards its ultimate aim, it was none the less necessary for the stating of the problem, and even for the furthering of its solution. The mission of founding the Universal Religion belonged of necessity to the West, for the requisite condition of such a mission was a military civilization in the midst whereof abstract science could arise. Abstract science, discovering the general and real laws of the various distinct orders of phenomena, is the only thing that can serve as the dogmatic basis of a doctrine capable of becoming truly universal; for such science reveals the fundamental order which dominates human existence, both individual and collective. This complete development of abstraction was, as Auguste Comte has shown, a special peculiarity of the military populations of the West; whilst again, this preponderant military activity was needed to allow of the establishment of the definitive religion; for it alone could implant the needful habits of initiative and personal independence. Thus, in short, the foundation of the Universal Religion could only have emanated from the West, the advance guard of Humanity, and it has indeed effectually emanated by the great construction of Auguste Comte, the final outcome as it is of all anterior evolutions. Thus, active relations of the West with the rest of the planet were indispensable, first for the establishment, and then for the diffusion of the Universal Religion.

Knowledge of the planet, not merely theoretical, such as astronomy furnishes, but practical, such as active exploration yields, was needed for the foundation of the definitive faith, to determine the exact position of the various peoples whom it was to bind in union.

In this way we form the conception of a truly world-embracing policy, avoiding the narrowness of the national standpoint, and the arbitrary vagueness of theological notions.

The scientific faith has thenceforth for its precise and sufficiently general object, to build up the unity of the world, by finally eliminating all concern for the supernatural and all empirical restrictions ; its all-embracing width of view never passing beyond the bounds of the real. Thus, the practical knowledge of our planet, completing the knowledge derived from astronomy, has furnished a foundation for the Universal Religion, by determining the precise object over which it was to exert its influence.

A real and thorough knowledge of the various civilizations on the face of our planet was necessary in yet another way for the foundation of the definitive faith ; for the spectacle of these manifold social evolutions helped to free men's minds from the habit of looking at things from an absolute standpoint, and to shew them how powerless theology is to found a Universal Religion. For the two great monotheisms, Islamic and Catholic, the only religions that lay claim to universality, were never able, in their periods of full ascendancy, to reach more than a minority of the human species. Lastly, the knowledge of these various civilizations could alone supply decisive verification of sociological laws, by allowing us to verify, in space, the laws of evolution discovered chiefly by consideration of the homogeneous series, in time, of the phases of Western civilization.

On all these various grounds then, it was necessary not only for the foundation, but also for the final establishment of the definitive faith, that there should be active relations between the West and the rest of the planet. A knowledge of the different populations of the world was needed as a preliminary to the conception of a general plan for propagating the doctrine elaborated by the group of Western peoples which are the flower of the human species. The relations that have been established between the West and the rest of the world, during the five centuries of the revolutionary era, were therefore as indispensable as they were inevitable.

But these relations could not but partake of the anarchical character of the era which witnessed their rise and development. A blind

empirical proselytism was eager to spread over the rest of the world
a faith which was gradually dying out in its own home.   These
attempts, often prompted by honorable feelings, in spite of the intellectual
narrowness on which they were based, were accompanied by oppressive
and gain-seeking measures on the part of Western powers.   This
oppression and pursuit of gain was only too much favoured by the
growing anarchy of the peoples, amongst whom the powerlessness of
the old doctrine and the absence of a new, left a clear field for the selfish
and aggressive propensities.

The first duty of the Positive Faith will be to regulate those
relations, which otherwise would be given over to the most ignoble
greed.   .

Before setting forth the principles of such a policy, especially as
regards China, I must first tell you, Gentlemen, very briefly, what
those relations were and are.

The ancient Greeks and Romans had only a very dim knowledge of
China, and their relations with her were never other than indirect ; and
this continued to be the case throughout the middle ages, when the Mussulmans were the principal intermediaries between the West and the Far
East ; and these intermediaries had an interest in concealing from both sides
the means of intercommunication.   Nevertheless some direct communication did take place ; and every one has heard of the celebrated travels of
Marco Polo.   These travels were performed from 1271 to 1295, in the
reign of Kublai.   Marco Polo himself has given us a very interesting
account of his journeys, highly instructive as regards the geography
of the middle ages.   A great many translations were made of his work,
especially into Latin, the original having probably been written in the
Venetian dialect.   Although his descriptions of the immense empire of
China were at first treated as fable, and brought the veracity of that
remarkable traveller into grave suspicion, they were nevertheless highly
important.   The recollection of a great Empire in the furthest East
remained as an object for the active investigation of the West to
explore.   From the 16th century onward the relations of the West with
China became much fuller and closer.   Opened by the two great
enterprises of Vasco de Gama and Christopher Columbus, those relations,
favoured by circumstances, grew increasingly active.   Westerns then

made their appearance in China in a passing and accidental way, but their appearance was that of greedy bucanneers and daring filibusters. This impression, long maintained, was only momentarily counterbalanced by the admirable mission of the Jesuits, the real glory of that celebrated society, and the most rational and moral attempt hitherto made to establish relations between the West and the rest of the world. And not only was the inception of this mission due to social motives, unlike the other enterprises which sprung from purely selfish aims, but more than all, its work was performed in a wisely relative spirit; as far as—perhaps even further than—the absolute spirit of Christian theology allowed.

The Jesuits thought, as many minds in Europe still think, that Christianity is the highest expression of human civilization; and that consequently it is a duty to share it with all the other populations of the earth. The various Christian missions were undertaken under the promptings of this most honourable sentiment, though the hope that they would succeed was altogether illusory. But the Jesuit mission in China was carried out with an exceptional degree of wisdom, and a fullness of devotion which will always command the respect of sensible men. We shall now give a brief account of it.

This great mission was inaugurated by father Matteo Ricci, (born at Macerata, in the marches of Ancona in 1552, died in China the 11th May, 1610); and it was marked from the outset by all the characteristics which it preserved throughout the seventeenth and eighteenth centuries. From the first he perceived the expediency of influencing specially the leading men, and above all the Emperor himself. He gave up the garb of a Buddhist monk, which he had at first assumed, and made the members of his mission adopt that of a Confucian literate instead. By many this conduct has been found fault with; but it was in reality full of wisdom, since his object was to bring the Jesuits into closer contact with the class which really controls China, and to sever all connection with the Buddhist priests, who were more or less looked down upon by the better educated class of the Chinese. And this measure was rendered all the more necessary, by reason of the great dogmatic resemblance that exists between Catholicism and Buddhism. Ricci instituted a system of wise toleration of the worship of ancestors and of the sky, and even of the worship of Confucius, which constitute the fundamental basis of Chinese civilization; lastly, he recommended Western civilization to China by propagating the teaching of abstract scientific knowledge; the feeble development of which constitutes in China the deep defect of its civilization.

This mission, then, was spontaneously established, as far as the mental narrowness of Christian dogma permitted, with the characteristics which are suitable to every wisely constituted mission; namely, appreciation and respect for the civilization which is to be modified, and services rendered in filling up by devoted and pacific propaganda the lacunæ which exist in it.

The mission thus instituted by Matteo Ricci was carried on in the same spirit and on a larger scale during the seventeenth and eighteenth centuries. By the astronomical and geometrical knowledge of the missionaries it rendered real services to Chinese civilization, without being able to effect, however, any deep reaching modification. To do that belongs to the Positive Religion alone. The Jesuits were always appreciated in China, so far as regards the Western scientific knowledge they introduced. The Emperor Kang Hi, by an ingenious experiment which I have already mentioned, obtained a proof of the superiority of Western over Chinese astronomy. Jesuits were thereupon placed at the head of the Mathematical Board; a fact which sufficiently demonstrates that the Chinese are by no means absolutely opposed to the dissemination of Western science, when proper respect is shown by its progagandists for the civilization of the Celestial Empire.

The mission of the Jesuits may be divided into two successive periods—the one extending over the seventeenth, the other over the eighteenth century—which may be conveniently termed, the former the Italian, the latter the French period. The first witnessed the foundation under the auspices of Ricci, the second was distinguished by the production of great learned works, especially those of Father Gaubil, who was its most eminent representative.

Besides these services to China, the Jesuits rendered to the West the important service of at length making known the greatness and civilization of China, by publishing immense works of learning; works which will always be for Western scholars the foundation for new investigations in this field.

And the Jesuits had the inestimable advantage of living their whole lives amongst the people they were studying. They thus were saved from forming those superficial estimates, often calumnious and always absurd, so frequently indulged in by passing travellers who pretend to judge of a civilization of which they can perceive nothing at first but the drawbacks.

We are indebted to Father Gaubil for a History of Chinese astronomy, which, owing to his profound astronomical knowledge and his intimate acquaintance with Chinese, he alone perhaps could have written. We also owe to him a translation of the Shu King, the most ancient and most valuable of the sacred books of China, and the study of which even to the Chinese themselves is beset with difficulties.

" The style in which the Shu King is written," says Abel Remusat, " savours of the period in which the book was composed; its excessive " brevity of expression, the choice of words employed, the sort of meta- " phors we find in it, make it beyond comparison the most difficult " of all Chinese books to read; and one might be able to read all " other books, even those of Confucius, and yet be unable to read and " understand this. It is in some sort a distinct tongue; differing " more from modern Chinese than that differs from any other " idiom."

Father Gaubil composed a great number of other works, all distinguished by deep learning and sober judgment. Sent to China in 1723, he died there the 14th July, 1759.

Besides his learned works, and his special labours as a missionary, Father Gaubil succeeded Father Parenin as Director of the College to which the young Manchus repaired to study Latin, in order to be afterwards employed in the conduct of affairs with the Russians. He was, moreover, interpreter for the Latin and Tartar languages. Many other Jesuit missionaries were able thus to combine the duties of their special mission with learned labours and important public functions, worthily fulfilled to the great advantage of the populations they sought to convert. Thus worked and spread, during two centuries, a mission alike useful to China and the West.

But however wise and praiseworthy in the main was this system of toleration towards the cult of Confucius and ancestors, it was nevertheless incompatible with the dogmatic narrowness of Catholicism, which the Jesuits had been able, by a noble politic instinct, to surmount. Abbé Boileau, exclaiming, "My Christian brain is turned," gives artless expression to the incongruity of the relative spirit and of a judicious toleration with the absolute dogmatism of Christian monotheism. The Papacy, therefore, owing to the perpetual agitation of the Dominicans, and faithful to the spirit of its dogma, at last condemned the system of toleration introduced by the Jesuits, the only system which could have allowed—not indeed of the chimerical conversion of China to Christianity—but, at least, of the admission of that creed to a footing of equality with Buddhism. None the less is it true that this great mission constitutes the only serious and honorable attempt to modify Chinese civilization.

The West will yet certainly be able to surpass this mission as regards the mental point of view, by basing itself on a relative and more real doctrine; but never, I venture to say, will it surpass the probity, the devotion, and the modesty of those worthy ministers of religion. It is but a duty of acknowledgment to pay so deserved a tribute of respect to this noble mission, the true title to glory of the Society from whose ranks it was recruited.

From the eighteenth century the commercial relations of the West with China became more extensive and important, but at the same time the disposition grew among Westerns to regard China as a mine to be worked to the utmost, without limits other than those interposed by insurmountable necessity. This they carried so far as to regard themselves as free from any sort of moral obligation towards these people; the only appeal was to brute force, and the West vaunts itself over a people who have virtually attained to the pacific and industrial stage, principally on the grounds of the superiority of its weapons of destruction. This disposition was specially displayed in the shameful opium war of 1842. In that expedition a powerful people was seen employing violence to coerce a Government into allowing its subjects to be poisoned; a sight dishonorable not merely to the English aristocracy and middle classes, who were the authors of it, but to the whole

H

West, on which recoils the blame of not having protested with sufficient firmness against so immoral an employment of brute force.[1]

Thus Western commercial relations with China became more and more subversive of order, mainly by reason of their protection by public force. They may be improved, when governments come to understand the need of correcting their abuses, instead of allowing them to take their course at the pleasure of public opinion, only too much inclined to favour such misdoings. For, under the guidance mainly of the so-called progressive school, it has come to such a pass in the West, that oppression and the exploiting of the other peoples of the world has been reduced to a system, under the specious pretext of spreading civilization. There has grown up with respect to China, and Western relations with her, a set of opinions which I must try to describe. These opinions are summed up in a proud feeling of the mastery of Western civilization, and a blind contempt for all other civilizations whatever. From this there results the disposition to introduce everywhere, and especially by means of force, under the empty name of progress, the mental anarchy and unregulated industrialism which are becoming more and more prevalent in the West. I may quote here two passages bearing on this subject, which are all the more significant, as emanating from sober and honorable minds. They will show to what a pitch of mischievous error men may be led by this vague and henceforward so dangerous a notion of *progress*, which in fact is now nothing more than a systematic glorification of an ill-ordered industrialism.

In a highly interesting work on Buddhism, M. Barthélemy-Saint-Hilaire sums up the opinion of a Chinese pilgrim about India, and follows it up by some observations of his own. " Yüan Chwang indicates " in a few lines the distinction of castes, and he dwells, as usual, upon " the four principal ones, only because it would take too long to give a " detailed account of the others, as he himself says. He gives a short " analysis of the laws of marriage amongst the Indians, and he takes

---

[1] In spite of vague economic maxims about free trade, it is certain that it has become the duty of every government to prevent a cultivation and commerce such as that of opium. By taking some such action, the West could show to the East the superiority of its civilization, instead of presenting the spectacle of public force placed at the service of unprincipled and unbridled greed.

" care to note the horror they have of a woman marrying a second time.
" Once a woman is married, she is expressly forbidden, for the rest of
" her life, to have a second husband. We know that this law, sanctioned
" by inflexible usage, has been perpetuated to the present day ; and quite
" recently the English papers in India have told us, as a quite unpre-
" cedented fact, and as a great victory over inveterate prejudices, that a
" young Hindu widow had just been married a second time. This is an
" immense step of progress which the English authorities have achieved
" after great efforts, and of which they are as proud as of having at length
" suppressed the atrocious custom of Sati."—(Barthélemy-Saint-Hilaire:
Buddha and His Religion, p. 257.)

Here was a custom which all sensible men in all times had been
pleased to respect. In all countries the state of widowhood has been
held in honour, as being a more perfect state than that of second
marriage. It has always been held that there was something worthy in
this faithfulness unto death. The Westerns come to India, and they
account as the greatest step of progress, the fact that they succeed in
destroying an honourable custom, which at all costs they ought to have
treated with respect. This is a truly characteristic example of the strange
infatuation of the Western mind, which leads it to extol as progress the
violation of some moral rule which should be extended instead of
repressed, merely because such a rule is not in keeping with the present
anarchical state of our civilization.

A protestant clergyman published, some time ago, an interesting
work on China, animated by the most benevolent feelings towards that
nation, which he had closely studied. He sums up in a few lines the
way in which, as he conceives, the West may civilize China :—

" If some hope may be formed of a change for the better, it should
" be based not on a more or less organized agitation, but upon this fact,
" that thought is beginning to circulate amongst the people. New ideas
" have been infused into the popular mind. Since the establishment of
" free intercourse with foreigners in 1842, the schoolmaster has been
" abroad in China. The spirit of self-reliance, so manifest in the last
" insurrections, has begun to take among the people a more elevated
" tone. Such commotions, like storms and hurricanes, purify the
" atmosphere. Movements of so grave a nature call forth thought and

" efforts; teach the people to act for themselves, and to throw down the
" fossil debris of prejudices, bigotry and superstition. Every shock in
" the nation reveals the working of this vast laboratory in which new
" and unexpected results are being prepared. We cannot help believing
" that all these moral undulations of the soil of China will result in
" producing something good. It is thus that our entire globe, after the
" terrible convulsions of nature had swept over its surface, ended by
" presenting an appearance which the sovereign Creator himself was
" pleased to pronounce good."—(*Rev. W. Milne: Real Life in China.*)

Let us remark, to begin with, in passing, how singular it is to hear
a minister of the Christian religion talking about superstition and
bigotry in connection with a civilization so free from supernatural
beliefs, properly so called, as Chinese civilization is. But what is, at
bottom, the ideal which it is thus proposed to introduce into China?
It is simply a state of complete anarchy, which it is hoped may some-
how finally eventuate in a regeneration of which neither the spirit, nor
the conditions nor the nature are at all defined.

And this is all the more characteristic from the fact that this
deplorable revolutionary jargon emanates from a man of order, from the
minister of a religion of peace, who all the better on that account does but
give involuntary expression to that disposition, which is becoming more
and more preponderant in the West, to consider every vague agitation
as constituting a step of progress.

To state the matter briefly, the West has opened up indispensable
commercial relations with China, but it has imported into those relations
a truly anarchical and oppressive tendency, by its continual appeal to
public force to back up, instead of to restrain, the most culpable
excesses of commercial greed; whilst those who sincerely desire the
amelioration of China by its contacts with the West, unfortunately bring
nothing but the narrowest prejudices to the appreciation of a civilization
which they completely misunderstand, and their only conception of what
is required for the civilization of that vast oriental empire is indeterminate anarchy. Their civilizing process consists in applying the
vague notion of progress, which, oftener than not, is but a synonym
for anarchy, and which is becoming more and more a cant formula for
justifying the most foolish enterprises.

An urgent need exists, therefore, for laying down the general principles of a more rational and a more moral policy which shall at length regulate relations which have arisen spontaneously from the unregulated activity of the West.

We must now rapidly indicate what are the fundamental principles in accordance with which the relations between the West and the rest of the planet should be regulated, and then we shall have to apply these considerations to the special case of China.

The past has, in the West, developed all the human forces under all their various aspects. This long and laborious preparation is now come to an end. The normal state ought to regulate the forces which the past has developed. It is this regulating function which the demonstrated religion inaugurates. For all the truly regenerate this regulating process should begin at once in all the various phases of private and public life. But from the social point of view, the most general relations, that is to say those of people to people, having been the first to be troubled, ought to be the first to be regulated, at least in their main scope. These general relations, troubled since the opening of the fourteenth century, are those over which we have most power, especially the extra-occidental relations, inasmuch as the usages with which they are connected are at once fewer and less confirmed. It is in the ordering aright of these relations that Positivism will be able from the very outset to make its superiority manifest; because it alone can conceive them without doctrinal bias whether in the direction of disparagement or admiration; and because it, at last, comes to regulate them in a moral, not in an arbitrary way; in accordance with principles based upon the whole range of the abstract branches of knowledge.

The universal religion, the final problem of which is to make sociality prevail over selfishness in all the various aspects of our existence, has at length laid down the principles of such regulation. But the preliminary question is, what, in the West, are the forces upon which Positivism can rely to constitute that public opinion which will make the general principles of the demonstrated morality prevail against the disturbing forces fostered by the revolutionary state? The forces to which Positivism can and ought to make its appeal to support, of their own free opinion, the prescriptions of the demonstrated morality are, essentially, women and the working classes.

Positivism lays down as a principle that morality is one; and that its prescriptions must be applied to all relations whatsoever, even to those between man and the animals; as indeed has been spontaneously admitted by the practical instinct of the West. Two classes are naturally disposed, apart from all dogmatic belief, by virtue of their nature and of their position, to admit and sanction this great principle; namely women and proletaries. For these classes necessarily suffer from an unregulated condition of the human forces, a condition which is invariably due either to the theoretical or the practical classes who, from the very fact that they constitute the directing forces of society, are always prone to abuse. The very characteristic of every true force is its liability to abuse.

As regards women, their tendency is to give a spontaneous support to all moral regulation, by reason of that pure and noble disposition which is part and parcel of their moral superiority; hence it is rather by virtue of their better inward nature than of their situation that they are naturally disposed to sanction all true rules of morality. Thus, in England, where the extra-occidental relations have received their most anarchical development, we have seen English women giving the effective support of their opinion to the abolition of negro slavery in the colonies. That admirable instance shows how great is the power they will be able to exercise when their noble spontaneous aid is extended to all moral regulation.

On the part of the proletariate the support will be less spontaneous and more systematic, as arising rather from the situation of its members than from their very nature. Every disturbance in the action of the social forces reacts necessarily, and with special force, on the immense mass of working men who form the very foundation of our societies. Now there is a close interdependence between all kinds of regulation; and those who demand the moral regulation of the relations between capitalists and workmen cannot approve of the anarchic domination of force in the relations of the West with the rest of the planet; and those of them, on the other hand, who, to gratify their greed or their pride, approve of the oppressive domination of the West, are in no position to demand from their chiefs a better administration of the social forces, power or wealth. It is to these two great classes, then, that Positivism, apart altogether from questions of dogmatic belief, makes its appeal to give their active sanction to the maxims of universal morality in their application to the most general relations of Humanity. It is for women and working men, guided by the incontrovertible demonstrations of the positive religion, to form at length in the West a preponderant opinion which shall put a rein on the disturbing forces that are taking advantage of the revolutionary interregnum to use public force in the service of private greed.

It is in this way that we shall form, by degrees, that current of opinion which is to moderate the disturbing elements issuing mainly from the middle classes which too often bring upon other peoples of the planet embroilment and oppression. But this opinion must and in the end undoubtedly will, receive effectual support from governments, more particularly from absolute governments.

For this disorderly action of the advanced populations upon the Orient tends to develop in the West an anarchical conception of progress, and this misconception, in its turn, serves as a justification in advance for any sort of disturbance whatever. The only notion of progress that now prevails in the West is that of an uncontrolled and limitless material development. What is now aimed at is to produce much and to consume more; that is deemed to be the one thing needful. Any modification whatever, especially if it be of the practical kind and disturbing in its effects, meets with instant welcome. It is progress! The notion of progress has actually become a sort of mechanical unreasoning justification in advance of any occurrence whatsoever, provided it brings with it some disturbance of the existing state of affairs. If you would like to keep things as they are, in scientific, in industrial, or in political matters, you are set down as retrograde; but if you want to disturb some established order, then you are progressive! The growing preponderance of such a notion as this is becoming more and more a source of danger. It is in the name of such a principle that the most anarchical attempts are being made, or at all events conceived, in science, in morals, in politics. Let some incompetent mind, without in any way fulfilling the preliminary conditions, make an attack on some most incontestable principle of science, his performances, the outcome of a wayward vanity, generally allied with profound mental weakness, instead of meeting with the contempt they merit, are hailed with applause by a still more incompetent public in the name of progress. The word is becoming henceforward a kind of mystic explanation in itself, dispensing with any need for reflection. Past, present, future, this wonderful word explains every thing, and thus it is that it has settled down into a common place dogma, as immoral as it is absurd.

It is high time to set our faces against this dangerous notion, which would compromise the existence of all order whatever. *Progress is only the development of order. Moral progress is more important than intellectual progress.* Such are the two great principles laid down by August Comte; and it is under the guidance of these principles that Western minds can be at last brought back to the normal situation, from which they now tend more and more to swerve. *Progress* must be held subordinate to *order; the supremacy of moral progress* must be at length proclaimed. Such are two of the essential conclusions resulting from the vast body of thought worked out by Positivism; and though these principles required the most mighty meditative efforts for their systematic establishment, as scientific truths they will win an ever-increasing sanction from common sense. Women and workmen will feel the profound danger of progress conceived independently of order; and the immense inconveniences of the supremacy of material over all other kinds of progress.

From Western governments, too, support may, on good grounds, be expected. Absorbed, as those governments are certain to be, in the problem of maintaining material order—a problem that is becoming more and more difficult in the midst of a growing mental and moral anarchy—they will before long come to perceive the solidarity that knits material order with moral order. They will soon perceive what tremendous danger there would be in developing, by an unsettling action upon the East, the disturbing notion of progress in vogue in the West. And even if it be true that our overt political intervention would be actually useful to the East, still the demoralizing reaction upon Westerners which such intervention undeniably produces would be enough to make us refrain from it, and confine ourselves to simple commercial relations, freely accorded on both sides and freely accepted.

It will be necessary, in short, that the public force should regard itself as bound to regulate, and at times even to restrict, instead of blindly fostering, the relations of the West with the East. It is in this sense that a change must be brought about in the opinions of peoples and of governments.

I should remark, that it is necessarily from the middle classes that these elements of disturbance emanate; and it is parliamentary governments, middle-class organs that they are, which especially favour and foster such a policy. .Moreover, it is in England that this line of extra-occidental policy finds its complete development. Thanks to its parliamentary regime, a portion of the English middle class has been able to make use of a haughty aristocracy to back up and to direct military expeditions for the purpose of opening up, by any and every means, fair or foul, outlets for their trade. The effect of such a course of policy is to impede the regulation of the industrial forces and to demoralize even the working classes themselves by making them parties to the exploiting of the rest of the planet for profits. This policy, too, has always had the unfailing support of journalism, which is but the necessary complement of a parliamentary regime. We have seen the most respectable organs of English journalism calling out for systematic massacre of the Hindus, and, to attain their end, inventing the most monstrous calumnies. Against these sanguinary outbursts some noble protests have been made in England. But Western journalism as a body has not raised its voice against such blameworthy diatribes.

It is in public opinion then, and in governments, especially strong personal governments, that will make themselves its organ, that we shall find a fulcrum for energetic reaction against an extra-occidental policy that is fraught with harm.

To begin with, in the special case before us, public opinion must undergo a profound change in its way of looking at Chinese civilization. It must recognize that there, some stupid prejudices notwithstanding, is a respectable civilization, of which the determining conditions ought to be understood before any attempt is made to modify it. There must be a recognition too, of the fact that the West has to get itself started in the way of making its escape from a profoundly revolutionary condition in order to arrive at a condition really normal, before it takes upon itself to modify other civilizations. Any such modifications, by reason of their indeterminate character, can only have a disturbing influence upon the peoples acted on, and a demoralizing influence on the peoples who attempt such action.

Chinese civilization has developed itself gradually and steadily in one determinate direction for some four thousand years. It presides over the destinies of one-third of the human species, enabling them to live respectable lives and in circumstances in many ways preferable to those enjoyed by a large section of the working classes of the West. This civilization, truly organic and firmly founded on an admirable family system, presents a spectacle from which the superficial revolutionary conceit of the West has some lessons to learn. Rightly placing, themselves at the normal point of view, the Chinese hold that continuity must be accepted as the basis of all social development; and that the present, born of the past to prepare the future, should first of all respect and honour the past instead of reviling and misunderstanding it, with an ingratitude as immoral as it is senseless. This great empire, too, in the course of last century, at length reduced to order the Tartar peoples; brought them at last into connexion with its own civilizing centre. China thus fulfils the function which a superficial view assigns to Russia; and assuredly fulfils it better than Russia could.

This great civilization, then, enables one-third of the human species to live peaceful lives,[1] without opposing to reforming influences any

---

[1] "I should be disposed to add my own testimony," says Sir George Staunton, "to the same facts and in the same spirit. In the course of our journey through "the Chinese empire on the occasion of that embassy, I can recall to my recollection "(the seaport of Canton of course excepted) but very few instances of beggary or "abject misery amongst the lower classes or of splendid extravagance amongst the ,' higher."

J. F. Davis then proceeds to quote the characteristic words of a Chinese, Tien Ké Chi, explaining his reasons for felicitating himself that he was born in China. J. F. Davis follows up the quotation by the following comments of his own :—

"The country cannot, upon the whole, be very ill-governed whose subjects other really serious resistance than that which results from a well-founded distrust of the truly anarchical guise in which Western civilization presents itself. Although the West has within itself a development of the social forces which indefeasibly confers upon it the supreme initiative, it is none the less true that those forces, unregulated as they are, are the cause of a profoundly anarchical state of things, the action of which upon China cannot be other than disastrous. Let the West solve, in short, the problem of its own moral organization. Until it shall have done that, the directors of Chinese civilization can only contemplate, with more aversion[1] than sympathy, a restlessness that grows more and more convulsive, and the reaction of which upon their own society could only promote disorder. Are we to introduce our disregard of all authority, our family system in such decay that proper respect for the paternal power is becoming the exception rather than the rule, into the

---

"write in this style. But it is a still more remarkable fact that the following is "a popular maxim of the Chinese, and one frequently quoted by them:—'To "'violate THE LAW is the same crime in the emperor as in a subject.' "—(China: by J. F. Davis.)

[1] "Some years ago I was in close friendly relations with a young Chinese "literate whom the desire of seeing Europe had brought to Paris. He was an "unreserved admirer of our modern scientific discoveries, photography, galvanism, "the marvels of electricity. But, in the main, he hardly envied us anything "beyond the positive results of our sciences: the moral side of our social condition "gave him anything but a favourable impression of us.

"He freely acknowledged the superiority of our intellectual enterprise, without "being at all persuaded that it was a thing for which we were to be envied.

"'The eyes of your intelligence,' he used to say to me, 'are more piercing "'than ours, but you look so far that you do not see about you.

"'You have a bold spirit, which must make you successful in many things; "'but you have not enough respect for what deserves to be respected. This "'perpetual agitation in which you live, this constant want of diversion, clearly "'indicates that you are not happy.

"'With you, a man is always as if he were on a journey; whereas we like to "'be at rest. As to your governments, I am willing to believe they have some "'good in them; but if they suited you as well as ours suits us, you would not "'change them so often as you do. I am quite sure to find, when I go back to my "'country, the same institutions as when I left it; and I see that not one of you "'would guarantee me for even a couple years the solidity of your government as it is "'to-day.' "—(China in presence of Europe: by the Marquis d'Hervey-Saint-Denys.)

midst of a civilization solidly supported on an admirable organic constitution of the family? It is easy to understand, then, the well-grounded repulsion felt by this people against closer contacts with the West. And the most exact and searching scientific analysis must sanction the feeling, and must at the same time proclaim, in the name at once of reason and morality, the need of restricting such contacts instead of enlarging them.

The regenerated West will have, without doubt, to exercise, later on, a pacific action, as salutary as it will be thorough, on this great civilization, in order to found the normal state of the human species on our planet. It will be of use, therefore, to indicate the defects inherent in this civilization, which our gradual action on it will supply, in order to constitute at length Humanity.

The main defect, the one which from the mental point of view dominates all the others, is the absence of the social institution of scientific abstraction. Concrete observation and science have been amply originated and extensively developed in China, but not abstract observation and science. Thence the absence of sufficient generalization, and the impossibility of a true mental systematization. Generalisation, like systematization, is the result of scientific abstraction, and can result from that alone.

But the mental constitution of China will furnish, as indeed I have already indicated, an admirable opening for the gradual introduction and admission into it by its directing minds, of that vast abstract construction which is the glory of the West, and the foundation of its final supremacy. And the possibility of this achievement will be due wholly and solely to the fact that science, co-ordinated, finds its ultimate outcome in morals, as is shown by the incomparable systematization of Auguste Comte. We admit, as do the Chinese thinkers, that theoretical speculation, like practical activity, should be subject to moral sway. But it can readily be shown, in accordance with this very principle, that, from the stand-point of theory, as well as from the standpoint of practice, what is required for an efficacious constitution of morals is precisely a long abstract preparation proceeding by successive stages from Mathematics to Morals. (Mathematics, Astronomy, Physics, Chemistry, Biology, Sociology, Morals.)

For it is the business of morals to establish the government of human nature on the basis of a thorough knowledge of it. Now knowledge of human nature, to be really thorough, must rest on the knowledge of the actual laws of the various phenomena by which it is influenced. How is it possible to know Man without knowing the laws, statical and dynamical, of the phenomena of Society? And how can these phenomena themselves be adequately understood without a knowledge of the laws of Life? And are not these in their turn dependent on Chemical phenomena, just as the latter are on Physical phenomena; which again operate under the influence of Astronomical phenomena, and finally of Mathematical? But if abstract knowledge of the laws of the various distinct phenomena is indispensable for a sound scientific theory of human nature, it is not less so for the establishment of the governance of it. For the power of modifying depends, as much as does the possibility of systematizing, upon the knowledge of abstract laws.

Thus it is, then, that the mental constitution of Chinese civilization, in spite of its immense deficiency, nevertheless presents an opening through which the regenerated West will be able to introduce into it modifications as salutary as they will be deep reaching.

From the family point of view, the West has, as regards the filial and paternal relations, more to learn from China than to teach her. In accepting, under this head, a truly organic constitution, all we shall have to do will be to systematize it. As regards the conjugal relations, the incompleteness of China's military development has kept them in an imperfect state. But, in this respect, and in the name of the universal perfectionment acknowledged by the school of Confucius as the final aim of human existence, it will be an easy task to bring about the full adoption of monogamy; of monogamy pushed to the extent of perpetual widowhood. Indeed the respect universally paid to widowhood in China will render such a transformation easy.

From the social point of view the Chinese have, more fully than the West, arrived at the truly normal state, that is to say at the regime of industry and peace; in so much that even their military activity is reduced to the pure normal function of gendarmerie. But the division between masters and workmen, the necessary base of all industrial systematization, has hardly been developed in China, except in a very insufficient way, more particularly as regards its agriculture, in which the system of very small holdings is almost universal: so that the normal constitution of the industrial and pacific state can finally arise only in the West: and on the other hand the lack of abstract science has not allowed of the establishment in China of industry on the grand scale finally founded on the use of machinery; so that the mental defect of this civilization has constituted a profound material defect. Under this aspect, again, industrial systematization, which necessarily rests upon the division between capitalists and workmen and upon the allied use of machinery, could not have its beginning any where but in the West, under the impulsion of regenerated science carried at length to religious height. But this systematization, once it has begun, will gradually obtain admittance into a civilization which acknowledges the fundamental principle of the normal preponderance of industrial and pacific life. Until that time shall have come, every premature attempt to transport into China our Western type of vast concentrations of capital, and of developed use of machinery, can have no other effect but to produce frightful perturbations.[1] Indeed the spectacle of our

---

[1] "All arrangements capable of contributing to the maintenance of order and " general tranquillity are made with admirable care.

"There is, in short, a business-like character about the Chinese which "assimilates them in a striking manner to the most intelligent nations of the " West, and certainly marks them out, in very prominent relief, from the rest of " the Asiatics. However oddly it may sound, it does not seem too much to say, " that in everything which enters into the composition of actively industrious and " well organized communities, there is vastly less difference between them and the " English, French and Americans, than between these and the inhabitants of " Spain and Portugal.   *   *   *   .

"We shall see that they have some ingenious contrivances by which to avail " themselves of the natural moving powers,   *   *   * but of the strength of " steam they are ignorant, etc.

"*Whenever the effects of our scientific machinery in abridging labour are* " *explained to an intelligent Chinese, the first idea that strikes him is the disastrous* " *effect that such a system would work upon his over-peopled country, if suddenly* " *introduced into it, and he never fails to deprecate such an innovation as the most* " *calamitous of visitations.*"—(*China: by J. F. Davis, formerly the East India* *Company's Superintendent in China.*)

own industrial anarchy is not such a seductive one as to incline Chinese statesmen towards any such premature and disastrous introduction.

To sum up, then; let us respect this great and noble civilization. Let us at length understand that, if it presents some unquestionable defects, our only hope of being able to remedy them lies in setting out with a thorough knowledge of the society in which it exists. The actual state of that society, the outcome of its whole past, must be taken as the starting point of a systematic and gradual modification. Let us admit henceforward that the West itself ought to find its way out of its own state of anarchy; ought, in short, to be regenerated; ought, in the main, at least, to have arrived at the normal state, before attempting any serious action upon China. Let us, in short, acknowledge that our attempts at forcible action upon this great people can only disturb them and demoralize ourselves. Let us await with respectful sympathy the further spontaneous evolution of this grand civilization, and in the free intercourse incident to commercial relations let us be able to divest ourselves of truly childish prejudices and to comprehend the noble aspects of an organization by which one-third of our species is directed in a fitting way. It is by thus bringing to our judgments a rational and moral disposition that the commercial relations now subsisting with China will spontaneously prepare the way, by her free and voluntary acceptance, of that action upon her which the regenerated West will then be worthy to exercise.

THE END.

B. MEIKLEJOHN & Co., PRINTERS, 26 WATER STREET, YOKOHAMA, JAPAN.

www.ingramcontent.com/pod-product-compliance
Lightning Source LLC
Chambersburg PA
CBHW030605270326
41927CB00007B/1058